The

Talking
GOD

To Torri Lord
May the Lord
cause you to
hear His

Dr Joyce ♡

DR. JOYCE R. WALLACE

SCEPTRE MINISTRIES INTERNATIONAL

First Printing: 2019

ISBN: 978-0-578-21854-0

Sceptre Ministries International
1200 NW South Outer Road Blue Springs, MO 64015
PO Box 53, Blue Springs, Missouri, 64114
www.sceptreministries.org

Also by Joyce R. Wallace
Meditations From The Book Of Esther

Printed in the United States of America

Dedication

This book is lovingly dedicated to the memory of all the beautiful people who have touched my life in a special way.

CONTENTS

ACKNOWLEDGEMENTS

I am grateful for family and friends who have inspired me in this endeavor. These are my husband, John, my daughter, Jai, the Friends of Esther and the Men of Mordecai. A special thanks to Chavos who continually encouraged me and to Claudia who functioned in an editorial capacity, providing the assistance I needed to complete the process.

INTRODUCTION

A few years ago, I was invited to do a teaching series at a local church. The pastors asked me to teach a course on becoming more skilled in hearing and recognizing God's voice. Encouraged by the response I received at that church, the next year I presented the lessons to a group of ministry leaders in California. Their enthusiasm and the encouragement of friends and family have resulted in this manuscript. The content has been expanded significantly from the original material. The basic themes, however, have not changed. Worksheets have been included in order to enhance the learning process and provide the opportunity for practical application.

The Talking God is a book that can benefit the new believer, who is just learning to hear the voice of God, as well as the more mature Christian. Even some people who have been Christians for several years still struggle with discerning the voice of God. However, hearing the voice of God is fundamental to our growth as Christians because it helps to reinforce the idea of a personal relationship with Him.

The process of learning to hear God's voice seems to be veiled in mystery. I believe that process can be simplified. This book contains principles and practices that I observe in my own life. The good news is that they work! It is my prayer that as you apply these teachings in your Christian walk you will experience similar results.

It is my desire that you will gain several things from time spent with this book. First, I hope you will recognize that God is not silent. *God speaks*! He desires to speak to and with each of us. Hearing the voice of God is not based on reaching some spiritual plateau or being some great man or woman of God. Everyone can hear. If you accept this, it will release faith in your heart to believe that God not only can, but, *will,* speak to you. God will speak to you because He wants you to know His will.

The next benefit to be derived from reading *The Talking God* is greater clarity in understanding how God communicates with you. It is possible that God is already speaking to you and you haven't recognized it. You will become more aware that God actually speaks to you in a specific way.

Studying this material will also help you to see the connection between seeking God and hearing His voice. We often make hasty entrances and exits into the presence of God during our devotional times. Our busy lifestyles rarely allow us the time to just linger in His presence. Seeking God in prayer is a good thing, and when we take the time to wait quietly in His presence it shows that we are ready to hear what He has to say. The Father heart of God yearns for a people who will zealously cherish His presence and the sound of His voice.

Learning to hear the voice of God involves canceling out other deceptive voices that bring confusion. You can learn to discern God's voice even in the midst of competing voices. There are four sections that cover this subject rather extensively.

I have included some worksheets as a point of focus in your study time. These are described below.

Speak Lord is a worksheet that you will find in several places throughout the book. It provides a focus for you as you are learning to hear from God.

Pause and Reflect is found at the end of each chapter. It is a question and answer section and gives you the opportunity to review your learning. It is designed to encourage dialogue and offers suggestions for further study.

Hearing from God is a worksheet to be completed after chapter four. It is a very basic tool to help you identify how God speaks to you. Appendix 2 has an extra copy this worksheet.

Hopefully, as you apply these teachings, you will learn to dialogue with the talking God and will be able to teach others how to hear from God also. Freely share the things you have learned.

As a reminder, the Word of God as revealed in the Bible is the basis of all His communication with us. You are encouraged to spend time reading and meditating in the Word. This will bring balance and clarity to whatever you hear.

CHAPTER 1

The Incredible Talking God

And you said: 'Surely the LORD our God has shown us His glory and His greatness, and we have heard His voice from the midst of the fire. We have seen this day that God speaks with man; yet He still lives'. Deuteronomy 5:24

We serve a talking God. This is a simple but amazing truth. Let it sink into your heart and start you on an incredible journey that will allow you to encounter God in a very personal way.

If God is a talking God, it follows then that He must talk to someone. Would it surprise you to know that we are the ones with whom He desires to speak? It has *always* been His desire to communicate with us. One of the arguments that prophets, such as Jeremiah and Habakkuk, made against idolatry was that the idols did not possess the power of speech (Jeremiah 10:3-5; Habakkuk 2:18-19). Jeremiah and Habakkuk found it perplexing that the children of Israel would serve idols that lacked the characteristics that were so prominent in God, namely, the ability to hear, see, and speak. These characteristics enabled God to communicate on a very personal level with His people and set Him above all other gods.

MEET THE TALKING GOD

In the first three chapters of Genesis we are introduced to the talking God. (You may want to read these chapters before proceeding further). We meet a God who speaks in time and space (Genesis 1:3-24) and carries on a conversation with the other members of the Trinity (Genesis 1:26). He converses with the first man, Adam, and the first woman, Eve, who were created in His image and likeness (Genesis 2:16-19; 3:9-19). Being made in the image of God meant that if God could communicate with them, they also possessed the ability to communicate with Him. Adam and Eve were created with everything they would ever need to make this possible. They had ears to hear God's voice, intellect to comprehend His words and a voice with which to respond.

GOD WANTS US TO HEAR

Like Adam and Eve, we too, are well equipped to hear God's voice. John 8:47 gives the requirement for hearing from God. Jesus said, *"He who is of God hears God's words; therefore, you do not hear, because you are not of God."* This Scripture makes it apparent that every born-again believer can hear from God. And, yes, that includes you. You are not an exception to this rule. Get rid of the idea that only so-called super saints like the big-name televangelists, your pastor, or some other highly respected religious leader can hear from God.

THE LORD WANTS TO TALK TO YOU

I am reminded of a precious couple who spent much time in prayer and waiting on God. The husband was less sure of his ability to hear the voice of God. After every session of prayer, he would ask his wife, "What did the Lord say?" She would share the impressions that she had received in prayer. One day when he asked her the same question, her response was, "The Lord said He wants to talk to you."

The Lord does indeed want to talk to, and with, every one of us. There were only two people in the world after He created Adam and Eve and He wanted both to hear His voice.

FROM THE BEGINNING

Genesis 1:27-28 makes it evident that God wants to speak to us. We are told, *"So God created man in His own image, in the image of God He created him: male and female He created them. Then God blessed them, and God said to them..."* The order presented here is first creation, followed by blessing through speaking. Please note the importance of the word *"then"* in our Scripture. The word *"then"* indicates that God started talking to Adam and Eve immediately after He created them. This lets us know that the relationship that God envisioned with Adam and Eve was one with open dialogue.

God communicated with Adam and Eve, so He could reveal Himself to them. He wanted to commune with them. Commune is the word from which we get our word communication. There are several shades of meaning to this word. In addition to meaning to speak, it means to declare, to converse, to command, to promise, to warn, to threaten, and to sing. This suggests that communication with God was designed to be a method through which we would receive a revelation of both His heart, His emotions, His thoughts and His will.

AND GOD SAID

What, then, was the nature of the first communication that transpired between God and this first man and woman? Exactly what did He say to them? I would love to have been there! Unfortunately, the Bible does not tell us about their initial dialogue, but we do know that from Scripture that God did talk with them.

Exploring God's conversation with Adam and Eve will offer valuable insight into some of the specific things that happens when He speaks to us. As we examine what He said to them, it will help us understand why it is important for us to hear the voice of God.

GOD'S VOICE PRONOUNCES A BLESSING

The very first recorded words of God to Adam and Eve pronounced a blessing over them. *"Then God blessed them, and God said to them, "Be fruitful and multiply, fill the earth and subdue it: have dominion over the fish of the sea and the birds of the air: and over every living thing that moves in the earth"* (Genesis 1:29).

There are two ways in which we can interpret this blessing. First, we can recognize that there is a blessing in just being able to hear the voice of God. There was a time when only certain people could hear God's voice. I Samuel 3:1 says, *"And the word of the Lord was rare in those days: there was no widespread revelation."*

Praise God, we can be thankful that we are in a time of widespread revelation and can hear God's voice. Jeremiah prophesied, *"No more shall every man teach his neighbor, and every man his brother saying, 'Know the Lord', for they shall all know Me, from the least of them to the greatest of them,* says *the Lord"* (Jeremiah 31:34). Matthew 13:16 says, *"But blessed are your eyes for they see, and your ears for they hear."* Each time God speaks to us we receive a blessing. Even when His voice is corrective, we are blessed in that He does not leave us in error.

The second way to interpret this passage is to recognize that God loves to bless us. To bless means to pronounce some specific good upon someone. However, a blessing from God goes beyond the mere utterance of words. It contains the power to bring the pronounced blessing to pass. There are specific blessings that God wants to bestow upon our lives. Deuteronomy 28:1-14 contains an example of just a few of the blessings that He has already spoken over His people. When we fail to hear His voice, we are ignorant of the blessings that He has prepared for us. God's blessings are a sign of His favor and to experience them is to have His favor rest upon our lives.

GOD'S VOICE BRINGS A PROMISE OF FRUITFULNESS

The voice of God gave Adam and Eve a promise that they would be fruitful (Genesis 1:28). It was God's way of saying to them, "There are only two of you now, but My plan is that through you the whole earth will be populated." Wow! That should have shaken them up on the inside. From two would come so many!

You see, fruitfulness contains the idea of increase. It means that something else will be added to whatever we already have. We are told in 2 Peter 1:5-8, *"But also for this very reason, giving all diligence, add to your faith virtue, to virtue knowledge, to knowledge self-control, to self-control perseverance, to perseverance godliness, to godliness brotherly kindness, and to brotherly kindness love. For if these things are yours and abound, you will be neither barren nor unfruitful in the knowledge of our Lord Jesus Christ."*

The opposite of fruitfulness is to be barren. In biblical times, it was very important for a woman to have children. Psalm 127:4-6 supports this. It says, *"Like arrows in the hands of a warrior, so are the children of one's youth. Happy is the man that has his quiver full of them."* Therefore, barrenness was experienced as a great reproach and a sign of ill favor from God. Examples of women in the Bible who struggled with barrenness are Sarah, Rachel, Hannah and Elizabeth (Genesis 16:2; 30:1; 1 Samuel 1:6; Luke 1:7, 25).

The woman in Scripture is often symbolic of the church. Isaiah speaking to the nation of Israel said, *"Sing O barren, you who have not borne"* (Isaiah 54:1). As Christians, we may experience barrenness wherein we feel emptiness in our spiritual life. Perhaps we aren't experiencing the growth we desire or we may feel as if we are failing every test. When spiritual barrenness exists, it could reflect our failure to hear God's life-giving words spoken over us and to us. When God speaks to us, His words are like the breath of life.

Jesus says in John 6:63, *"The words that I speak to you are spirit, and they are life."* When Ezekiel was commanded to prophesy to the dry bones, he cried out, *"O dry bones, hear the word of the Lord"* (Ezekiel 37:4). God's promise concerning the dry bones was, *"Surely I will cause breath to enter into you and you shall live"* (Ezekiel 37:5). Psalm 119:107 says, *"I am afflicted very much; Revive me, O Lord, according to Your word."* The Psalmist's prayer acknowledges God's words as a source of life, energy and strength.

In 1 Peter 2:2, we are told that it is necessary to feed upon the word of God to experience spiritual growth. The Holy Scriptures will bring life to us as we hear and meditate upon what is written. When we combine the hearing of the word with obedience to the word, the outcome will be much fruit.

GOD'S VOICE GIVES UNDERSTANDING OF OUR PURPOSE

At some point in life, we all wrestle with questions relating to our purpose. God told Adam and Eve that they were put on the earth to populate it and to exercise dominion over it. He is the one who established their purpose in the universe. When Saul of Tarsus encountered Jesus on the way to Damascus, he asked, *"Lord, what do you want me to do?"* (Acts 9:6) Jesus spoke to Saul and gave him understanding regarding the call to ministry that was upon his life.

One thing we need to settle in our hearts is the fact that God has a purpose for us. He *really* does! Some of us will have a sense of this purpose earlier in life. For others, it may come in later years. The thing to remember is that the time we become aware of our purpose is not the time when God first has revelation of it. God has always known what He has destined for us. He told Jeremiah, *"Before I formed you in the womb I knew you; before you were born I sanctified you; I ordained you a prophet to the nations"* (Jeremiah 1:5). The words, *"Before I formed you in the womb I knew you"* could have been spoken over any one of us. God's purpose for us is established in His eternal existence. It is as old as the Ancient of Days, Himself.

In discovering God's purpose for our lives, we may have to inquire of Him, as did Saul of Tarsus. Questioning God is one way in which we can obtain more information about a matter. When we struggle with knowing why we are here and how our life is to make a difference in the world, we need to hear God's voice giving definition to us. God does not want us to be ignorant regarding His will. In Ephesians 5:17 Paul says, *"Therefore do not be unwise, but understand what the will of the Lord is."*

GOD'S VOICE DESCRIBES OUR SPHERE OF INFLUENCE

When God told Adam and Eve that they would have dominion over the earth, He was describing their sphere of influence. Their role, which was to influence the whole earth realm, was considerably different from that of all the other creatures that God made. Each of us is unique and God has so ordered our environment and life circumstances to fit in with His plans for us. The voice of God comes to us to reveal our place in the universe.

Adam and Eve were given the whole earth as the place of their influence. Most of us will not be given that kind of assignment. In 2 Samuel 18:1, we are told that David appointed captains over thousands and captains over hundreds. Jesus taught thousands but seemed to have His greatest impact ministering to the twelve disciples. Today with television, the internet and social media, there are many evangelists who minister to hundreds of thousands and even millions. Yet, the pastor who ministers to a congregation of fifty or a mother who attends her family of four are also given a sphere of influence. What we do in our sphere of influence, no matter how small it seems to us, impacts the kingdom of God. God will speak to us and increase our understanding regarding our sphere of influence.

GOD'S VOICE BRINGS PROMISE OF PROVISION

God spoke to Adam and Eve about His provision for them. He told them that He had provided certain herbs and fruit trees for their nourishment (Genesis 1:29). He wanted to make sure that they were well sustained and not worried about how they would survive. The voice of God comes to reveal and release His provisions for us in all areas of our life. Knowing this can free us from unnecessary anxiety. Jesus said, *"Do not worry about your life, what you will eat or drink: nor about your body what you shall put on...for your heavenly Father knows that you need all these things"* (Matthew 6:25a; 32b).

GOD'S VOICE CLARIFIES OUR CALL

When God spoke to Adam, He gave him a job description. Adam was placed in the Garden of Eden and his job was to cultivate it and keep it. We could call him a gardener, though after his sin it seems his job description was expanded to farmer. Jesus called Peter and Andrew from the fishing trade to become fishers of men (Matthew 4:19). God told Ezekiel that he was called to be a prophet and gave him information regarding the responsibilities of that office (Ezekiel 2:1-10). These examples indicate that God does not want us left in the dark regarding our life's purpose or how we are to function in it. He wants us to know why He created us and desires to use us to bring honor and glory to His name. God graciously supplies us with all the information we need to effectively fulfill His will.

GOD'S VOICE INSTRUCTS

God established rules to govern Adam's conduct in the garden. He said, *"...Of every tree in the garden you may freely eat: but of the tree of the knowledge of good and evil, you shall not eat, for in the day you eat of it, you shall surely die"* (Genesis 2: 16-17). This Scripture brings comfort because it lets us know that the voice of God will instruct us. Isaiah 30:21 reinforces this saying, *"Your ears shall hear a word behind you, saying, "This is the way, walk in it," whenever you turn to the right hand or whenever you turn to the left."* God's voice will keep us on the right track and alert us when we are about to derail.

God was both Adam's creator and his teacher. Jesus was often referred to as a Rabbi or Master Teacher. Holy Spirit was sent from the Father to be our teacher today. Jesus said, *"However, when He, the Spirit of truth has come, He will guide you into all truth: for He will not speak on His own authority, but whatever He hears He will speak, and He will tell you things to come"* (John 16:13).

GOD'S VOICE AIDS IN DECISION MAKING AND SETTING LIMITS

Adam and Eve were told how to make right choices. The voice of God comes to teach us how to make decisions in conformity with His plan for us. In Deuteronomy 30:19 God spoke through Moses to the children of Israel saying, *"I have set before you, life and death, blessing and cursing; therefore, choose life, that both you and your descendants may live."*

God helps us to make choices that please Him by establishing limits for us. He not only tells us what we are to do, but also what we are not to do. He set boundaries or limits for Adam and Eve. He did this by clearly informing them about dietary choices that met His approval and what choices would meet with His disapproval. He continued to do the same with the children of Israel through the various laws He established. You can read about some of these laws in Leviticus. God sets limits for us to provide spiritual boundaries and to create a safe environment in which we are to order our lives.

GOD'S VOICE BRINGS CORRECTION

Earlier, I stated that the voice of God is a blessing even when it brings correction. Correction, or discipline, is part of a parent's responsibility to a child. Since God is our heavenly Father, He will let us know when we do something that grieves His heart. Deuteronomy

8:5 says, *"You shall know in your heart that as a man chastens his son, so the Lord your God chastens you."* Proverbs 3:11-12, echoes a similar message; *"My son, do not despise the chastening of the Lord, nor detest His correction. For whom the Lord loves, He corrects, just as a father the son in whom He delights."* God wants us to please Him in all we say and do and correction is one of the methods through which this is accomplished.

Adam's and Eve's disobedience, made it necessary for God to discipline them in order to bring them back to their purpose. Sin distorts the purpose of God in our lives. It prevents us from seeing things from a divine perspective. The voice of a loving Father brings His children back from the path of disobedience to the road of righteousness.

GOD'S VOICE GIVES US HOPE

After Adam and Eve had sinned, God told them of His plans for restoration and redemption. Disobedience is often followed by guilt and feeling rejected by God. The enemy uses this to try to bring division between us and God. God informed Adam and Eve of the consequences for their disobedience, yet, He was also quick to give them hope regarding redemption. He provided a covering for their nakedness and gave them a promise concerning Christ, the Redeemer, who was to come (Genesis 3:15-21). Jesus foretold Peter's denial, and at the same time conveyed a message of hope. He informed Peter that He had prayed for him to be sustained by his faith (Luke 22:31-34).

Even in our weakest moments or times of great failure when we feel we have blown it again, God will speak a word of encouragement to our hearts. The eyes of God see us where we are and the voice of God calls us to where He is. David asked himself, *"Why are you cast down, O my soul? And why are you disquieted within me? Hope in God"* (Psalm 42:5). We can find strength to continue in difficult situations because the voice of God brings encouragement and hope.

SUMMARY

We serve a talking God who desires to speak to us. The importance of being able to hear the voice of God has been illustrated through examining the content of His first conversation with Adam and Eve. From that conversation, the various functions His voice serves in our lives became clear. When God speaks to us He bestows a blessing upon us, helps to understand our purpose, describes the sphere of our influence and gives us a job description. His voice is also a means whereby we are taught by Him, pointed toward wise choices, made aware of certain limits and given correction. Lastly, the voice of God offers words of comfort and hope. Of course, this list is by no means exhaustive. It does, however, provide some guidelines regarding what we can expect in communication with God.

PRAYER

Dear God, I want to hear your voice. Teach me how to know when You are speaking to me.

PAUSE AND REFLECT

Please read the first three chapters in Genesis.

What do you think it was like for Adam and Eve to hear the voice of God for the first time? Go through the Bible and find some other examples of when God spoke to people for the first time (Ex, Moses, Saul of Tarsus, Abraham Nathaniel). How did each of them react to hearing the voice of God?

Review the ten functions of the voice of God. Explain them in your own words.

In which of these functions has it been difficult for you to hear God's voice?

In which of these functions has it been easier for you to hear His voice?

What has God spoken to you through this chapter? Write it here.

Tell how you will use the information in this chapter.

QUIET TIME: BE STILL AND KNOW

Ask yourself: "What blessing is God speaking over me right now?" Write it down.

CHAPTER 2

Holy Communion

And there I will meet with you, and I will speak with you from above the mercy seat, from between the two cherubim, which are on the ark of the testimony, about everything which I give you in commandment to the children of Israel. Exodus 25:22

GOD SPEAKS

We serve a talking God who desires to talk with us. One of the most picturesque passages in the Bible is found in Genesis 3:8. It describes the voice of God as *"walking in the garden in the cool of the day."* This is a beautiful expressive picture of the relationship God had with Adam and Eve. In the quiet of the day's end He would come into the garden for a personal encounter with them. Most commentators agree that there is something about the language in this Scripture that suggests that this was the usual occurrence. God's way of drawing near to Adam and Eve was through His voice. The sound of His voice was like approaching footsteps.

Adam and Eve knew God's voice and were accustomed to holding conversations with Him. This is evident from the fact that when He would ask them questions they would respond. Talking with God was a part of the regular routine of their daily life. It was as natural as living in the garden and flowed effortless from their relationship with Him.

God's communication with Adam and Eve was an essential part of their natural development and their spiritual growth and maturity. It served as a bonding experience between them. They were the crowning glory of His creation and He took great pleasure meeting them in the garden at the end of the day. As God conversed with them, they learned more and more about Him. He revealed Himself to them through His words and His presence.

I WILL COMMUNE WITH YOU

God made this promise to Moses, "*I will commune with you*" (Exodus 25:22). God had given Moses instructions regarding the construction of the tabernacle and all its furnishings. This, of course, included the Ark of the Covenant and the Mercy Seat. The Mercy Seat was the lid or top of the Ark of the Covenant. It was made of acacia wood and overlaid with pure gold. In Hebrew, the word for Mercy Seat relates to the dual idea of being a covering as a top or lid and also to pardon or atone as in covering a debt. On top of the Mercy Seat were two gold cherubim, one at each end. Their wings came together and spanned or overshadowed the Mercy Seat. Underneath their wings was where the high priest would sprinkle the blood of atonement once a year.

Built into the tabernacle with its elaborate furnishings and symbols, which are shadows of heavenly things, was a place for God to communicate with His people. The place where God would speak with Moses was above the Mercy Seat.

Moses probably listened in awe as God gave him the details for constructing the tabernacle. That sense of awe must have increased as Moses was told about the Ark of the Covenant that would eventually hold the Ten Commandments. Add to that the mystery of the Mercy Seat covering the Ark of the Covenant and symbolically containing the revelation of a God who is full of mercy. But there was more! Then God gives Moses the most amazing promise; "*And there I will meet with you, and I will speak with you from above the mercy seat, from between the two cherubim, which are on the ark of the testimo-*

ny, about everything which I give you in commandment to the children of Israel." (Exodus 25:22)

What an amazing promise! Clearly God was saying, "Moses, if you build it, I will come."

DRAWING NEAR TO GOD

The Mercy Seat became the speaking place or the place of communion. It was where God would share His heart with His servant. Moses would enter the Tent of Meeting and stand before the Ark and God would speak to him (Numbers 7:89). God would share His heart with him and Moses would come to know God in the most intimate way, face to face (Exodus 33:11).

Under the Old Covenant the thought of approaching a holy God was very intimidating. However, through the Mercy Seat the people were given a revelation of a God who tempers justice with mercy. Hebrews 4:16 extends to us the same invitation that God originally gave to Moses. We are invited to *"come boldly to the throne of grace, that we might obtain mercy and find grace to help in the time of need."* This is an open invitation to come into God's presence and commune with Him.

CHOSEN TO COME NEAR

The cross is the Christian's Mercy Seat. From Calvary's cross God's love for the world was revealed as Jesus hung there. Through His death, we are now brought near to the Father of all Mercies (Ephesians 2:13). We are brought near that we may know Him in an intimate way.

Psalm 65:4 says, *"Blessed is the man You choose, and cause to approach You, that he may dwell in Your courts."* In times past this privileged blessing of drawing near to God was reserved for the Old Testament priests, but under Christ we have all been made *"kings and priests unto our God*" (Revelation 5:10). God is the One who draws us into His presence. Sometimes it may seem as if the responsibility is on us. Not so! We cannot even come to Him unless He draws us (John 6:44).

And draw us, He will. As we hunger for the words of His mouth, He will pour them forth. God validates our hunger and desire to know Him by filling us with treasured words from His heart.

We can come near to Him in full assurance of faith (Hebrews 10:22). We can approach Him with the expectancy that He will be available to us. Jesus says in Revelation 3:20, "*Behold, I stand at the door and knock. If anyone hears My voice and opens the door, I will come in to him and dine with him, and He with Me.*"

JUST TALKING

Jesus spent lots of time with His disciples. We would call it quality time. Quality time is the phrase that has been coined to describe time spent with people we love and care about. It is time given which is free of distractions and the other person receives full attention.

Quality time spent with the Master meant that the disciples were afforded the opportunity to observe Him as He preached, taught, performed miracles of healing and saved the unsaved. They followed Him along the seashore, on the hillside, in boats, to the garden of Gethsemane and eventually to Calvary. Do you think these were quiet times? I really don't think so. They probably had hours and hours to converse with Him.

Can you imagine talking with Jesus into the wee hours of the morning? What would it be like to share some humorous event and have Him join you in laughter? Does the idea of having Him share His most intimate thoughts with you excite your heart? Can you imagine Him calling you by name or simply addressing you lovingly as,

"Friend"? These were some of their cherished quality time experiences.

Jesus was always eager to dialogue with them. They were comfortable with asking Him to expound on something they did not fully understand. Sometimes, He would initiate a dialogue with them after an extensive teaching session or after something disturbing had transpired. There were times when He would pull certain ones aside and share at a deeper level about His mission and purpose. Sometimes He would comment on something He had observed about them (Matthew 17:1; Mark 5:37).

THAT I MAY KNOW HIM

Paul cried out in desperation and holy longing in Philippians 3:10, *"That I may know Him."* Paul's desire was to be fully acquainted with the nature and character of Christ.

Yes, Jesus talked with His disciples. There was so much that He needed to share with them about His mission and how they were a part of God's eternal plan. Heart to heart talks were a natural part of their relationship. The disciples probably never entertained the idea that Jesus would **not** talk to them. It was mutually expected and because it was expected, it happened.

When He conversed with them He was modeling aspects of the intimate relationship He had with the Father. He indicated that He talked often with the Father and at one point said, *"Father, I thank you that You always hear Me"* (John 11:42). The Father would speak words of encouragement, approval and validation to His Son (Matthew 3:17, John 12:28). There seemed have been an intense longing within Jesus for fellowship with the Father and He would devote entire nights to prayer and communion with Him.

We can enjoy that same kind of relationship with Jesus that the disciples experienced. God will reveal Himself to us as we set aside time to be with Him. Perhaps we need to pull away from the many things that compete for our attention and serve the purpose of distracting us from His presence. In His presence, He will speak His word into our heart. The more we hear His words, the greater the desire to hear. Let us embrace His words as the bread of life that feeds us spiritually.

SUMMARY

The Bible reveals that God is not only willing to speak with us, He *longs* to have communion with us. He wants to bring us to a place of where He shares with us one-on-one. Hearing His voice can become a regular part of our day. These conversations with Him become the place of holy communion.

PRAYER

God, my heart's desire is to know You and to be intimately acquainted with Your thoughts and Your ways. Please give me the desire of my heart. Amen

PAUSE AND REFLECT

Research further the meaning of the Mercy Seat. For example, what is the symbolism of the materials from which it was constructed?

Read Hebrews 4:16. What does it mean to approach the throne of grace with boldness? Do you expect to find mercy from God? Is there a part of you that secretly fears the wrath of God? Is your approach to God filled with guilt and shame?

Choose some incidents from the Gospels in which Jesus dialogued with His disciples. What were the topics of His conversations with them? What was their response?

Read Revelation 3:20. How does God knock at your door?

Have you heard the term "spiritual intimacy"? What does it mean to you?

What has God spoken to you through this chapter? Write it here.

Tell how you will use the information in this chapter.

QUIET TIME: BE STILL AND KNOW

Why does God say He wants to commune with you today? Write it down.

CHAPTER 3

How God Speaks

"For God may speak in one way, or in another." Job 33:14

We serve a talking God and He is multilingual. Part of our growth and maturity as Christians is related to the extent we can become fluent in God languages. We must recognize the many languages of God because He will speak to us in one or more of these languages. The languages He uses when speaking to you is what I have termed as your God languages. The language He uses most often with you is your primary God language.

God uses languages to make Himself known. On the day of Pentecost when the disciples received the baptism of the Holy Spirit they spoke in various languages. The multi-cultural crowd that heard them marveled that they could speak in languages which they obviously had never learned. Because of this, the crowd gave glory to God because they heard the wonderful works of God proclaimed in their native tongue. This dramatic example, which is recorded in Acts 2, shows how God used language to reveal Himself to people.

Since God reveals Himself through language, we must look to Him to teach us how to understand His language. The more we understand His languages, the more growth we will experience in our knowledge and understanding of Him.

God wants to expand and increase our fluency in His languages. One reason for this is so that we can be more effective in our ability to minister and share the gospel with others. Many of the disciples were uneducated, yet we have seen in Acts 2 where they were used by God to speak a foreign language. This opened the door for them to begin to witness to the crowd in Jerusalem about Jesus as Messiah.

Our Scripture at the beginning of this chapter states that God has spoken in various ways. In this chapter, we will explore some of the ways in which God speaks. As we explore this topic, remember, that no matter how God chooses to speak to us, He must also interpret, that is, give us understanding of what He has spoken.

GOD SPEAKS THROUGH HIS WORD

Romans 15:4 says, *"For whatsoever things were written before were written for our learning, that we through the patience and comfort of the Scriptures might have hope."* There have been times when someone has approached me and said, "God does not speak to me." I would smile and then ask him or her, "Can you read? Do you have access to a Bible?" The answer is always, "Yes" to both questions. My next response is, "God has already spoken and continues to speak. All you need to do is read your Bible and you will start hearing what He wants to say to you."

Can you see how God has provided a way for us to hear His voice and to become familiar with His will and plan for us? It is through the written word, the Holy Bible. Scripture is the most powerful and dynamic of all the languages of God. His word is timeless and consistent. It is the truest truth in existence.

The Scriptures become the foundation for whatever method God uses when He speak to us. It is through the written word that we can verify or test any communication attributed to God. No matter what language God uses, it will line up with what He has already said in the written word. If it does not, you must question the source.

Some biblical scholars make the distinction between two primary Greek words that are translated "word" in the New Testament Scriptures. These words are *logos* and *rhema*.

The term *logos* refers to the totality of the Word of God as well as of the person of Jesus Christ. Examples of references to logos include John 1:1, Philippians 2:16, Hebrews 4:12, and 1 Peter 1:23.

By way of contrast, *rhema* is applied to the spoken word. Holy Spirit breathed words seem to be the essence of the meaning of rhema. Note the occurrence of this term in Matthew 4:4 where it says, "*Man shall not live by bread alone, but by every word* (rhema) *that proceeds out of the mouth of God.*"

Rhema seems to have reference to a specific portion of Scripture in the Bible that speaks to your heart through the inspiration of Holy Spirit. That Scripture would be for your personal application. This could be a Bible verse that engages you because it has relevance for a present situation that you are encountering.

 Peter and Mary are examples of persons who had a rhema experience. When Peter denied Christ, the Scripture says he "*remembered the word* (rhema) *of Jesus*" (Matthew 26:75). Rhema is the term Mary used when responding to the angel Gabriel after she was told she would bear the Christ child. She said, "*Let it be to me according to your word (*rhema)" (Luke 1:38). Hopefully, from this example you will get the sense of the personal nature of rhema. Rhema, simplified, is the voice of God that comes to you in the present moment.

Other instances of the use of rhema occurs in Romans 10:17 and Ephesians 6:17.

GOD SPEAKS THROUGH DREAMS

Dreams are the images that occur to us during our sleep. Our emotions and thoughts are a part of the dream process. We are sometimes prone to dismiss the content of our dreams as the residue of a stressful day, an overactive imagination or having eaten spicy food.

Of course, these things can affect our dream-life. However, discounting your dreams can cause you to overlook this important channel of communication that God has provided.

Dreaming is one of the oldest languages of God and is documented in the Old Testament. God communicated with Jacob through dreams (Genesis 37: 5-11). God directed ungodly men through dreams (Genesis 40:1-7, 41:1-7, Daniel. 2:1). Examples of dreaming also occur in the New Testament. Joseph, the husband of Mary, was given specific instructions in a dream regarding precautions to take which would ensure the safety of the Christ child (Matthew 2:13, 19). When Jesus was on trial, Pilate's wife had a dream and warned her husband to be careful in rendering any judgement concerning Him (Matthew 27:19).

An important reference to dreams occurs in Job 33:14-18 where Elihu speaks to Job saying, *"For God may speak in one way, or in another, yet man does not perceive it. In a dream or in a vision of the night, when deep sleep falls upon men, while slumbering on their beds, then He opens the ears of men, and seals their instruction, in order to turn them from his deed, and conceal pride from man, He keeps back his soul from the pit, and his life from perishing by the sword."*

Dreams are not to be discounted for God will use them to speak to us. Even in our sleep states He will open our ears so that we can hear what He has to say. For some Christians dreaming is the primary way God speaks to them. I have a friend who finds it rare not to have at least one dream a night.

Obviously, God does not give every dream we dream. Ecclesiastes 5:3 addresses this; *"For a dream comes through much activity, and a fool's voice is known by his many words."* If you are a dreamer, be diligent to ask God for wisdom to discern whether the dream you had came from Him. On a personal note, the way that I know I have received a dream from God (dreaming is not my primary God language) is that I wake up immediately and I remember the dream clearly.

GOD SPEAKS THROUGH VISIONS

Dreams tend to occur when we are asleep and visions, by contrast, tend to occur when we are awake. Numbers 12:6 says, *"Hear now My words: if there is a prophet among you, I, the Lord, will make Myself known to him in a vision. I will speak to him in a dream."*

There are numerous instances in Old Testament Scripture that prove that God speaks through visions. Isaiah, Zechariah, Daniel, and Ezekiel are just a few of the Old Testament saints to whom God revealed Himself in a vision. Ezekiel states, *"The heavens were opened, and I saw visions of God"* (Ezekiel 1:1).

In the New Testament, there are several examples as well. Peter had a vision on a rooftop. God used that vision to deal with some of Peter's misconceptions to prepare him for another phase in ministry (Acts 10:9-15). The Apostle Paul had a vision of a man asking him to come and minister in Macedonia (Acts 16:19). John's prolific visions on the isle of Patmos are recorded in the book of Revelation.

Our idea of what having a vision is like is usually thought of being similar to watching something on a movie screen. This is true for some, but not necessarily true for all. It may be helpful for you to also think of visions as mental pictures. If I said the words "ice cream sundae" to you, a certain picture would come to mind. Sometimes visions are like that, coming in the form of pictures in your mind. When I realized this, I recognized that occasionally I do have visions. I have also had two or three visions that fit more with the traditional notion of what it means to have a vision.

DREAMS AND VISIONS: PROCEED WITH CAUTION

Since dreams and visions are often encoded, it is necessary to seek God for interpretation of dream symbolism. Joseph (Genesis 40:8) and Daniel (Daniel 2:14-28) understood the meaning of dreams.

Zechariah had lots of visions but did not always understand them. God sent an angel to reveal to him the meaning of his visions (Zechariah 1). God would not give a vision and then keep the meaning hid-hidden indefinitely. When God gives a dream or a vision, He will be faithful to give the interpretation as you seek Him regarding it (See Daniel 8:15-17).

At the same time, we must be very careful when it comes to dreams and visions and how they are interpreted. Keep in mind that the Bible is finished, and it tells us everything we need to know. When God gives a dream or vision, it must line up in agreement with what He has already revealed in the Scriptures. Dreams and visions should never be given equal or greater authority than the Scriptures. God's written word is the ultimate authority for Christian faith and practice. If you believe you have had a dream or vision from God, diligently pray about it as you examine it in the light of the written word. If it agrees with Scripture, then ask God what He wants you to do in response to the dream or vision (James 1:5).

If you are a dreamer or have visions, ask God to help you to understand what He is speaking. There are also some very good biblically based books available that with help you with interpreting the symbols in your dreams and visions.

GOD SPEAKS AUDIBLY

Many Christians profess to having heard the audible voice of God. This is when you can hear God speak out loud. Moses heard God speak in this manner. The children of Israel all heard God's audible voice. Matthew 3:15-17 records how Jesus heard the voice of the Father speak words of validation and affirmation to Him. In Acts 9, Saul had an experience of hearing Jesus speak audibly to him.

GOD SPEAKS THROUGH ANGELS

In Hebrews 1:14, angels are described as, *"ministering spirits sent forth to minister for those who will inherit salvation."* Sometimes God sends angelic visitors to communicate His will. Abraham (Genesis 18); Lot (Genesis 19); and Samson's parents (Judges 13) experi-experienced angelic visitations. Angels also appeared to Peter, Joseph, Mary and Jesus. Angels brought messages of impending danger (Matthew 2:13); commissioning for leadership (Judges 7); an announcement of God's blessing in response to prayer (Luke 1:1-12); judgment; (Genesis 19:12-13) or to explain something that was not understood (Zechariah 6:1-8). In addition, there were times when God would use angels to reveal His plans for a specific group of people (Luke 2; 8-15).

AUDIBLE VOICES AND ANGELS:
PROCEED WITH CAUTION

There is a tendency to elevate those who hear God speak in the more unusual ways, such as audibly or through angelic beings, to a higher spiritual status. Indeed, some who have heard the audible voice of God may even attribute to themselves a deeper spiritual relationship with God. If you have ever had such thoughts, it helps to remember what Paul said in Romans 12:3-8:

> *For I say, through the grace given to me, to everyone who is among you, not to think of himself more highly than he ought to think, but to think soberly, as God has dealt to each one a measure of faith. For as we have many members in one body, but all the members do not have the same function, so we, being many, are one body in Christ, and individually members of one another. Having then gifts differing according to the grace that is given to us, let us use them: if prophecy, let us prophesy in proportion to our faith; or ministry, let us use it in our ministering; he who teaches, in teaching; he who exhorts, in exhortation; he who gives, with liberality; he who leads, with diligence; he who shows mercy, with cheerfulness.*

The way God chooses to communicate with us individually or as a church or even as a nation is always a measure of the grace that is bestowed on us. This grace is not based on our works, but often happens in the absence of them. This to say, the one who hears the voice of an angel is not greater than the one who has a dream. And the one who has a dream is not greater than the one who hears God's voice in the logos. It is all by the grace of God, His unmerited favor given to us because of Jesus Christ.

GOD SPEAKS TO US THROUGH LIFE CIRCUMSTANCES

Abraham sent his servant on a mission to find a wife for Isaac (see Genesis 24). The servant wasn't sure how God would direct him to the potential bride, so he prayed. He asked God to orchestrate circumstances in such a way that he would know the woman who was destined to become Isaac's wife. Specifically, his prayer was, *"O LORD God of my master Abraham, please give me success this day, and show kindness to my master Abraham. Behold, here I stand by the well of water, and the daughters of the men of the city are coming out to draw water. Now let it be that the young woman to whom I say, 'Please let down your pitcher that I may drink,' and she says, 'Drink, and I will also give your camels a drink'—let her be the one You have appointed for Your servant Isaac. And by this I will know that You have shown kindness to my master"* (Genesis 24:12-14).

God orchestrated specific events and actions, so they transpired exactly as the servant had requested in his prayer. The servant had no doubt that the circumstances indicated God was speaking to him. God had revealed to him the bride He had chosen for Isaac.

Speaking through circumstances may be the way in which we have most been influenced by the voice of God. He just seems to show up in the routine of our everyday life. It is often in response to a quick prayer or some unspoken desire or just divine providence. God will use circumstances to make us aware of His will. We often say,

"Things just came together" and we take that as an indication that God has set His approval on a certain course of action. On the other hand, we may say, "For some reason, things just didn't work out" and we interpret this as God speaking to us to avoid a certain situation.

GOD SPEAKS THROUGH PROPHETS

One of the main ways that God spoke and made Himself known to the children of Israel was through prophets like Moses, Jeremiah, Deborah, Isaiah and John the Baptist, just to name a few. In Jeremiah 7:25 God said, *"Since the day that your fathers came out of the land of Egypt until this day, I have even sent to you all My servants the prophets, daily rising up early and sending them."*

There are prophets placed in the church today. Ephesians 4:11-13 states, *"And He Himself gave some to be apostles, some prophets, some evangelists, and some pastors and teachers, for the equipping of the saints, for the work of the ministry, for the edifying of the body of Christ, till we all come to the unity of the faith and of the knowledge of the Son of God, to a perfect man, to the measure of the stature of Christ."*

Modern day prophets are subject to the guidelines given for prophecy by Paul in 1 Corinthians 14:3. Paul says, *"But he who prophesies speaks edification, exhortation and comfort to men."* Simply speaking, edify means to build up, exhort means to urge or encourage, and comfort means to speak words that relieve stress or distress.

PROPHETS: PROCEED WITH CAUTION

There are two cautions that need to be mentioned regarding prophecy. The first concerns a tendency to want to run to some prophet to get a "word from the Lord". The worldly counterpart to this is to seek information from a psychic. This relates to depending on others to hear from God for you. We are not to use another's relationship with God as something we rely on to know God's will for us. Remember, this was the sin of the Israelites. Exodus 20:19 says, *"But they said to Moses, "You speak with us and we will hear; but let not God speak with us, lest we die."* God will sometimes use people to speak words of encouragement and affirmation into our lives. He will even use us to do the same for others. However, we are not to become the mouth of God for others, neither are they to become the mouth of God to us. God wants us all to know Him, from the least to the greatest.

The second caution is regarding how you respond to prophecy. Prophetic words come to confirm what God has already spoken to you. They must not be used to order your life apart from God's written word. All prophecy is to be judged and tested. A true prophet will welcome accountability.

GOD SPEAKS THROUGH JOURNALING

Journaling has become a very popular method for hearing the voice of God. Habakkuk was told to write down the vision plainly (Habakkuk 2:1). Journaling is very simple. Open your Bible and select a passage of Scripture to read. After prayerful meditation write down your spontaneous thoughts. In journaling, you are encouraged to hear what God is speaking to you personally about what you read. This is actually a way in which you can receive a rhema word.

When I journal I generally come to God with a specific concern or question. I use my journal as a place to dialogue with God. First, I write down my question or concern. Next, I spend time in prayer, reading the Word and waiting before the Lord and then more prayer. Next, I review my concern and write down the things that come to mind.

When I finish writing I do not read what I have written. Instead I put my journal away for two to three days or longer. The reason for this is so that when I come back later and read what is written I can be more objective. At that point I ask myself, "Does it still seem as though God was speaking to me or do I discern that it was primarily my own thoughts?" I am usually quite surprised at how clear God's voice came through.

RANDOM THOUGHTS

God invades our thought life to speak to us. For some Christians, this is a common occurrence. Sometimes when it happens, we don't always recognize that it was God speaking. Maybe you have not seen a high school classmate in ten or more years. From out of nowhere you have a thought about him. The next day you run into him at an unexpected place. Another example would be if you suddenly have an urgent thought to pray for someone. You later find out that they were in an accident. You may have a thought about cooking a certain meal. Your spouse comes home and tells you that was exactly what he or she wanted for dinner.

As we follow Paul's exhortation to have the mind of Christ (Philippians 2:5) we will become more sensitive to how God speaks through our seemingly random thoughts.

JOURNALING AND RANDOM THOUGHTS: PROCEED WITH CAUTION

God is not in every single thought we think. Journaling and random thoughts are subject to the same criteria of lining up with the Bible. Remember the enemy invaded Eve's thought life in the garden. Thus, all thoughts that came to her mind were no longer controlled by God. The enemy could now plant a thought there. Moreover, because she gained knowledge of good and evil she would have her own thoughts as well.

In journaling, it is easy to go off on writing tangents that are more self-expressions than God talking. These self-expressions are not necessarily to be devalued, but rather understood for what they are, **self-**expressions, expressions of our own thought life.

GOD SPEAKS THROUGH THE STILL SMALL VOICE

Elijah, the prophet, fearing that Jezebel would have him killed, escaped to a cave for protection (See 1 Kings 19). He had several unusual experiences while there. At one point, there was a strong wind followed by fire and then an earthquake. Elijah may have expected God to show up in all these manifestations, but God was not in any of them on this occasion. These were ways in which God had appeared to His people in the past. He sent a strong wind to dry up the waters of the Jordan. He appeared in fire and smoke on Mount Sinai. Isaiah 29:6 predicts that God will come with an earthquake.

When we are learning to hear the voice of God, we might expect Him to speak in some dramatic way. If He does not speak with a lot of drama or with great drum rolls, we may be disappointed. We may even say, "God has not spoken to me." Keep in mind that Elijah was a rather dramatic man; appearing and disappearing, calling down fire from heaven and starting and stopping the rain. It may have been his expectation that God would appear with some awesome manifestation. However, what he heard was a still small voice, which he recognized as the voice of God.

The still small voice is called the sound of gentle stillness. This reminds me of Psalm 46:10 where God encourages us to, *"Be still and know that I am God."*

The phrase "be still" means to let fall or to let hang down. It speaks of being relaxed and not engaged in activity, especially with the hands. When I think of this I form a mental image of a Raggedy Ann or Raggedy Andy doll wherein their whole body just goes limp.

We don't have to put forth fleshly effort or strain to hear. An invitation to *"Be still and know that I am God"* invites us to come to a place of calm assurance. It is the place where we rest in the Lord and trust Him to awaken His voice in us and to us. Then, we will not approach God with anxiety. We will rest in the knowledge that He is as desirous to speak to us as we are to hear.

We are God's children and His still small voice resides in us. In order to hear the still voice, we must slowdown from the frantic pace in which we are so accustomed to live. When our hearts become quiet in His presence and we meditate on the Scriptures, that still small voice gets stronger and stronger.

GOD SPEAKS MANY WAYS

Obviously, there are numerous other ways in which God can and does speak to us (Hebrews 4:1). The list discussed here is not by any means exhaustive. He can use a book, a sermon, a song, a painting, a movie or a teaching. Many times, He will use other Christians to speak His words of comfort and encouragement to us. Yet, we cannot limit God to **our** personal present revelation and experience. He is limited only by His word. His ways are beyond what our finite minds can fully grasp. The most we understand about Him is so small when we reflect on how big He really is. The more we know about Him, the more we realize how little we know.

The Bible is always our structure and frame of reference for any means by which God may choose to speak. In Galatians 1:8 Paul said, *"If we, or an angel from heaven, preach any other gospel unto you than that which we have preached, let him be accursed. As we said before, so I say again, If any man preach any other gospel unto you than we have received, let him be accursed."*

HOW DOES GOD SOUND

It is easy to get the voice of God confused with our idea of how God **should** sound. I really enjoy watching movies in which a "God-type" character appears. It's fun just to hear what the director imagines God's voice would sound like. There are some Scripture references that give us a clue as to how God's voice sometimes sounds.

In Revelation 1:5 John saw Jesus and gave this description, *"And His feet were like unto fine brass, as if they burned in a furnace; and His voice as **the sound of many waters**."*

Psalm 47:5 says, *"God is gone up with a shout, the Lord with **the sound of a trumpet**."*

And we read in Job 37:5, *"**God thunders** marvelously with His great voice…"*

Yes, God's voice can sound like many waters, a trumpet and even thunder. However, most often the voice of God sounds like our own voice. This is one of the reasons we doubt that we have heard from God. The idea of God's voice sounding like our voice does not fit in with our ideas about how God should sound. It just doesn't seem very spiritual, does it?

Interestingly, this is the same problem we have with discerning the voice of the enemy and the voice of the flesh. Most often, they, too, sound like our own voice. God not only speaks to us in our own language, He speaks in our own voice. Have you ever shared a prophetic word? Have you spoken a word of comfort or encouragement to someone? Whose voice was used? It was your own voice! Nothing took possession of you and controlled your vocal cords and gave your voice a totally different sound. Was God speaking through you? Absolutely! Well, He sounded like you!

SUMMARY

God is creative in the way He communicates us because His desire is to become a real and personal God to us. No matter how He chooses to speak, our reference point is always the written Scripture, the Bible.

PRAYER

God, I want to know my God language. Amen.

PAUSE AND REFLECT

Review some of the primary ways God speaks to us. It would be helpful to look up the Scripture context for these.

Why are some of the ways in which we hear God's voice followed by a word of caution?

After reading this chapter, are you able to identify the way in which God speaks to you?

Can you think of a time when God spoke to you in a clear concise way?

Practice journaling once over the next week. Use the Scripture, *"Be still and know that I am God"*, as a prayer focus. How does the Scripture apply to you? Write your thoughts here.

How do you plan to use the information shared in this section?

What has God spoken to you through this chapter? Write it here.

QUIET TIME: BE STILL AND KNOW

God speaks through the still small voice. What is He saying to you now? Write it here.

SPEAK LORD WORKSHEET
(Please refer to Appendix 1 before completing)

1. One thing that I would like for God to speak to me about is:

2. This is what I feel that God has already spoken to me regarding my concern:

3. It is important for God to speak to me about this area of my life because:

4. This is what I will do in response to what God tells me:

CHAPTER 4

Learning to Hear

"Now the boy Samuel ministered to the Lord before Eli. Now the word of the Lord was rare in those days; there was no widespread revelation. And it came to pass at that time, while Eli was lying down in his place, and when his eyes had begun to grow so dim that he could not see, and before the lamp of God went out in the tabernacle of the Lord where the Ark of God was and while Samuel was lying down, the Lord called Samuel. And he answered, "Here I am!" And he ran to Eli and said, "Here I am, for you called me." And he said, "I did not call. Go and lie down again." And he went and lay down again. Then the Lord called yet again, "Samuel!"

So, Samuel arose and went to Eli, and said, "Here I am, for you called me." He answered, "I did not call my son; lie down again." (Now Samuel did not yet know the voice of the Lord: nor was the word of the Lord yet revealed to him.)

And the Lord called Samuel again the third time. So, he arose and went to Eli, and said, "Here I am, for you did call me."

Then Eli perceived the Lord had called the boy. Therefore, Eli said to Samuel, "Go lie down; and it shall be, if He calls you, you must say, 'Speak Lord for Your servant hears." So, Samuel went and lay down in his place. Now the Lord came and stood and called as at other times, "Samuel! Samuel!" And

*Samuel answered, "Speak, for your servant hears." Then the
Lord said to Samuel..." 1 Samuel 1:1-11*

We serve a talking God. We can have conversations with this
talking God, but we must first learn to recognize His voice. It is not
unusual to hear someone ask, "How do you know when God is speaking to you?" The quick answer is, "I'm still learning." That's because
getting to know the voice of God is a learning process. As we apply
ourselves to this process we can become more proficient in knowing
when He is speaking to us.

TEACH ME O LORD

In Psalm 25:5 the Psalmist prays, *"Lead me in Your truth and
teach me, for You are the God of my salvation."* Learning to hear from
God begins with a simple prayer like the one quoted above. We are to
ask God to teach us to know His voice by sensitizing our hearts and
ears to hear Him when He speaks.

The Bible is a book about how God spoke to men and women
just like you and me. The record of what, when, where and how God
spoke to them is written for our learning. Hopefully, as you read the
Bible, you will receive faith to believe that if God spoke to them, He
can and will also speak to you.

The amazing thing is that God spoke to people from all walks of
life. Solomon was a wise king, Ruth was a field laborer, Amos was a
farmer, Jeremiah was a young lad, Peter made a living fishing and
Zacchaeus worked for an ancient IRS. God wasn't looking for a select
group of people with a certain profile. And then, "too bad for you" if
you didn't fit the profile. He wants us all to hear. Romans 2:11 says
"God shows no partiality."

WE LEARN TO HEAR

We start our journey in learning to hear the voice of God as babes in Christ. This means that we will make some mistakes along the way. If we are not discouraged by these mistakes, and continue, we will mature and become more sensitive in discerning when God is speaking to us. Hosea said, "*Let us know. Let us pursue the knowledge of the Lord*" (Hosea 6:3). Let's look at the story of the child Samuel as recorded in I Samuel 3:1-11. It provides a model for learning to hear the voice of God.

Samuel was in the tabernacle with Eli, the high priest. Apparently, at some time between midnight and 4:00 a.m. he was awakened by someone calling his name. We are told that the person who called Samuel was the Lord. We will now follow Samuel as he progresses from not knowing God's voice to recognizing His voice quite clearly.

The first thing we want to note is where Samuel was when God spoke to him. He was in the tabernacle. He was in the place where the presence of God dwelt, yet he was still unschooled in hearing God's voice. Similarly, we can be involved in church and church-related activities and fail to grow in our ability to recognize God's voice to us.

HEARING POSITION

For Samuel, being in the tabernacle puts him is in a position where he can hear from God. I call this his Hearing Position. The concept of having a Hearing Position is vital to the development of our hearing sensitivity.

Your Hearing Position is the place where you are or the activity in which you are engaged when God's voice comes through to you with the greatest clarity. Over the years, I've asked several people about this and they usually have a ready response. The answers were quite varied ranging from doing household chores to taking a shower to lying in bed waiting to fall asleep. Other answers were more conventional such as studying the Bible or in prayer. One of my hearing positions is in worship. When I enter worship it's like God says, "I have your full attention now." It is amazing some of the things that He has chosen to share with me during my public as well as private worship times.

YOU CALLED?

Samuel initially thought Eli had called him. This is not unusual. When we are just beginning to hear the voice of God, His voice may have a familiar sound and we may attribute it to someone else's voice. Usually at this stage we often mistake God's voice for our own inner voice. In this case Samuel thought his mentor, Eli, had spoken to him. Being a dutiful lad, he ran to the old priest and asked him what he wanted. Eli told Samuel that he had not called him. Samuel must have been rather puzzled and may have begun to doubt whether he had actually heard a voice. He could have dismissed it as his over active imagination.

WHO IS THIS ANYWAY?

When we are learning to hear God's voice, we will experience times of doubt and confusion. Perhaps you can identify with the following scenario. You have spoken with someone in person on several different occasions and have come to know their voice well. What happens when that person calls you on the telephone for the first time? You will probably have to ask, "Who is this?" only to be slightly embarrassed to discover it is someone you know. We may know the voice of God in certain contexts such as in reading the Bible or hearing a sermon from our pastors, and yet not be familiar with God's voice as it speaks in personal communication to us.

Eli told Samuel to go back to bed. Samuel obeyed and shortly thereafter the same thing happened again. He heard the same voice calling his name. He rushed to Eli and made inquiry, only for Eli to tell him again that he had not called him.

We may ask why this kept happening to Samuel. He must have felt rather foolish and maybe a little bit delusional. One possible explanation is that God would use this occasion to teach Samuel to recognize His voice. This should encourage us to realize that God doesn't give up on us when we don't get it right the first time. In Psalm 62:11 David said, *"God has spoken once, twice have I heard"*. God's voice came to David twice repeating the same thing. Sometimes God's word is repeated for emphasis. At other times, it is repeated simply because we didn't get it the first time. Since God wants us to know His voice, He will give us many opportunities to hear it.

HEARING ERROR: SPEAKER IDENTIFICATION

In the process of learning to hear God's voice we are subject to several hearing problems. I have labeled these problems "Hearing Errors". One common problem occurs when we hear what is spoken but do not identify God as the speaker. Little Samuel heard his name called several times but didn't know that God called him. This is like a story in John 12:27-29. Jesus was troubled about His impending crucifixion and prayed, *"Father glorify your name"*. The voice of the Father came from heaven saying, *"I have both glorified it and will glorify it again."* All the people who stood by Jesus heard the voice but there was disagreement over the source of the voice. Some said it was thunder and others said an angel spoke to Him.

Who you attribute as the source of the message will affect your response. Remember, God wants us to know His voice. On the occasion mentioned above, Jesus told them that the voice from heaven came not for His sake but for theirs. He already knew His Father's voice. They, however, were guilty of the first error, hearing God but attributing His voice to someone else.

HEARING ERROR: LACK OF UNDERSTANDING

The second problem that may be encountered in our early efforts to hear the voice of God is to know that God is speaking, but not understand what is being spoken. As alluded to previously, even Jesus' followers experienced this problem. He often taught lessons in the form of parables and they were puzzled by these mysterious spiritual truths. After the crowds disappeared, they would pull Him aside and ask Him the meaning of the things He taught. He would always patiently answer their questions because He wanted them to understand. This is just as true today as it was then; He wants us to understand His language. Proverbs 4:7 says, "*Wisdom is the principal thing; therefore, get wisdom: and with all your getting get understanding.*"

HEARING ERROR: HOW HE SPEAKS

The way in which the voice of God comes to us may give rise to doubt. There are probably an infinite number of ways that God could speak to us. In Hebrews 1:1 the writer said that God spoke at various times and in various ways. In other words, God has throughout the ages used various ways to communicate His will. We identified many of these in the previous chapter. Knowing **how** God speaks to us makes it easier to recognize **when** He speaks to us. He spoke to Samuel by direct voice and He continued to speak to Samuel by this means throughout his ministry.

HEARING ERROR: IGNORANCE OF SCRIPTURE

Ignorance of the Scriptures will interfere with our ability to hear. Jesus said, "*You are mistaken, not knowing the Scriptures nor the power of God*" (Matt. 22:29). God will always speak with us according to the written word, the Bible. As our knowledge and understanding of the Bible grows so will our ability to know when God is speaking to us. After Jesus' death, His disciples struggled with believing the report of the angels and other evidence that pointed to His resurrection. John gives a reason for this when he says, "*For as*

yet they did not know the Scripture that He must rise from the dead"
(John 20:9).

HEARING ERROR: NO COMMITMENT

Lack of commitment to the will of God for our lives is another way that opens the door to problems in hearing. Some people are afraid of God's will for their life. They remain "on guard" lest God tells them something they don't want to hear. Ezekiel was told to eat the entire scroll that was filled with God's words to him and the children of Israel (Ezekiel 3:1-3). He could not pick and choose as if at a buffet table. Jesus attempted to communicate with Peter about His impending death and resurrection, but Peter didn't want to hear it. Peter tried to quiet Jesus by protesting strongly that it would never happen. Jesus had to let him know that he was opposing the will of God for Him (Matthew 16:21-23). Peter was not able to come into agreement with the Father's will for the Son. Our desire to hear God speak to us must flow out of a commitment to do His will.

Some Christians stand in long prayer lines wanting to get a word from the Lord through the evangelist or pastor. When God doesn't speak to them they leave disappointed. I wonder how many words from the Lord over the course of their Christian walk have gone unattended. God has no need to speak to us any new thing until we have treasured what has already been spoken and applied it to our lives. A sign of our valuing God's word is that we follow through and act upon what He said.

SUMMARY

Learning to hear the voice of God is a process which often involves trial and error as it did with Samuel. The concept of the Hearing Position was introduced. The Hearing Position is the physical or spiritual place you are in when you can hear God's voice the clearest. In addition, several problems were described which could interfere with our ability to hear. These were called Hearing Errors.

PRAYER

Lord, I want to learn about You. Amen.

PAUSE AND REFLECT

In what way does learning to hear God's voice involve moving from the unfamiliar to the familiar?

Review the Hearing Errors that were described in this section. Explain them in your own words.

Rank the Hearing Errors, starting with the one you most challenging for you.

Tell what things could increase your potential for Hearing Errors.

What has God spoken to you through this chapter? Write it here.

Tell how you will use the information in this chapter.

QUIET TIME: BE STILL AND KNOW

Think about the Hearing Errors. Which one is God speaking to you about? What is He saying? Write it here.

HEARING FROM GOD WORKSHEET

(Please refer to Appendix 2 before starting.)

God has a language. How does He speak to you?

    A. Primary language

    B. Secondary language

What is your spiritual theme?

Describe your hearing position.

What is your hearing time frame?

What creates static?

How do you receive confirmation of what God has spoken?

CHAPTER 5

A Hearing Aid

"Sacrifice and offering You did not desire;
My ears You have opened..." Psalm 40:6

We serve a talking God who makes repeated attempts to engage us in dialogues with Him. This is evident in the story of Samuel wherein God called him three times. The third time when Samuel went to Eli, Eli finally grasped the spiritual significance of what was transpiring.

Eli gave Samuel some very clear guidance. His instructions offer us a wonderful model containing simple steps that anyone can follow in learning to hear God's voice. Eli's instructions, found in 1 Samuel 3:9 were, *"Go, lie down; it shall be, if He calls you, that you must say, "Speak Lord, for your servant hears."*

INITIAL STEP: GO

"Go", was the first word of instruction. Eli was aware that God did not speak to Samuel when the lad was with him. The voice came when Samuel was alone. So, the initial thing to do was to get Samuel back to the place where the voice had called him, back to his Hearing Position. "Go", is a word to get him moving in the right direction. It means to take that initial step.

If your desire is to start hearing the voice of God, what is the first thing that you need to do? Eli identified this for Samuel. The first step was to leave Eli. Leaving Eli, therefore, represents a transition for Samuel. Eli's voice will no longer be the primary way that he receives messages from God. He will move into a more personal and intimate relationship with Him.

You may have someone in your life who has functioned as an Eli. Perhaps they are very instrumental in your spiritual development. You may have become dependent on them to hear from God for you. Maybe this is the time God wants to start dealing with you in a more personal way. Are you willing to let go of the Eli in your life so you can hear God for yourself?

BE STILL AND KNOW

Eli told Samuel to "*lie down*." This is a command to enter the place of quietness and rest. It is the place where we learn to cease striving and straining to hear the voice of God. We learn to rest in the knowledge that we serve a talking God and He wants to talk to us. Psalm 46:18 tells us to "*Be still and know that I am God*." When we are still, we are quiet before the Lord without anxiety. It refers to a calm state of mind.

In our worship times we have gotten so used to working for everything and controlling things by our actions. When there is silence or inactivity in our corporate worship times we tend to get nervous. One of the tasks for the church leadership is to teach the people how to be still in God's presence. Preparation for hearing from God involves quieting our hearts and minds.

It requires discipline to bring our minds and bodies to a place of stillness before God. We have become so acclimated to living with high levels of noise. Ringing cell phones, blaring televisions, honking horns, cheering crowds, yelling referees, screeching brakes, flashing sirens, and many other sounds have become a normal part of our environment. We usually don't even notice the noise until it's time to be still.

Psalm 37:7 says, *"Rest in the Lord, and wait patiently for Him."* And in Psalm 40:1, David says, *"I waited patiently for the Lord: and He inclined to me. And heard my cry."*

Waiting patiently on the Lord, that is, waiting without noise in our spirits, has its own reward. David said that God *"inclined to him"*. This means God turned His ear to hear what David had to say. When you wait on the Lord, God will turn His ear in your direction. Knowing that God was listening brought assurance to David that God would respond to Him. God had heard his prayer and would answer his petition.

KNOW YOUR HEARING POSITION

At this point you may choose to go back and read the brief section on the Hearing Position in the previous chapter. God spoke to Samuel while he was lying down. This was his Hearing Position. As a reminder, your Hearing Position is the place where God's voice comes clearest to you. It will not necessarily be the same for each person. Eli encouraged Samuel to posture himself in the position he had when God called him.

BE EXPECTANT

Eli said to Samuel *"It shall be if He calls you"*. This would create an attitude of expectancy. Eli was encouraging Samuel to be listening for God's voice. To be listening for God to speak means we are waiting with open ears that are inclined toward the sound of His voice. Isaiah 55:3, says *"Incline your ear, and come to Me. Hear and your soul shall live."* Inclining the ear is the opposite of pulling the ear away as in not wanting to hear. An inclined ear is bent toward the speaker. This shows that the hearer is ready and anxious to hear the words of the speaker.

When Moses saw the burning bush that was not consumed by the fire, he stopped what he was doing and turned aside to see it. He turned away from all distractions that would interfere with his view. The inclined ear has been turned toward God's voice because of tuning out all other distracting sounds. This reflects our desire to hear God's voice over and above the other voices that vie for our attention. It is sharing the same spiritual hunger as Job had when he said, *"I esteemed the words of Your mouth more than my necessary food"* (Job 23:12). He considered God's words a valuable treasure that he guarded by holding them in the highest regard. They were his "necessary food" or appointed portion. Job was saying that in the same way that his physical body would be compromised if denied nourishment, his spiritual life would be compromised if He did not give attention to God's word.

PRACTICE RESPONDING

Samuel was told to respond to God. To paraphrase what Eli said, "If God calls you respond. Say something. Let Him know that you have been waiting for Him to speak to you." Eli was trying to teach him to respond to the first sound of God's voice.

Here are a couple of ways in which you can practice responding to God. For example, when you hear the word of the Lord through a sermon, ask yourself what would be the proper response to the message. Reflect on the last sermon you heard. What did you do? Was it dismissed as simply another good sermon? Did you think it could really help that couple sitting in the third row? Or did you see it as applicable to you and prayed for God to help you to walk it out?

Even in your private devotion and study time, make a response to things you read. It is so easy to make Bible Study about amassing more information. Try taking the approach that through His word God has something to say to you. What is it? How will you respond to His voice?

Luke 24:13-35 tells the story of two very disillusioned and discouraged disciples who were on their way to the town of Emmaus. Jesus had been crucified and their expectations regarding Him were dashed. At the time they were journeying to Emmaus, Jesus, had actually risen from the dead, but they were unaware of this. Jesus sought them out and joined them in their walk. As they walked together He showed them through the Scriptures how the prophets had accurately predicted the things that had happened. At a certain point in the journey Jesus made a gesture to indicate He was going to leave them. They responded to that gesture by asking Him to stay with them. He stayed with them and they continued talking and shared a meal together. This story lets us know that we must become accustomed to responding to even the slightest indication of His presence, whether it's coming toward us or moving away from us.

ASK HIM TO SPEAK

Samuel's response to God was, *"Speak, Lord, your servant is listening."* This expresses his desire to hear God's voice and is also a request or invitation for God to speak to him. In Song of Solomon 2:14, the Beloved makes an impassioned request to the Shulamite maiden *"Let me hear your voice: For your voice is sweet and your countenance is lovely"*.

"Let me hear your voice." This is God's appeal to us, His beloved. He says that the sound of our voice is pleasing to His ears. Therefore, whether it is in worship or strong tears of intercession or a whispered "I love you", God wants to hear our voice. He invites us to talk to Him.

We can contrast Samuel's eager attitude for God to speak to Him with that of the children of Israel. They told Moses, *"You speak with us and we will hear; but let not God speak to us, lest we die"* (Exodus 20:19). They were afraid of a personal relationship with God. Moses told them *"Do not fear"* (v.20). Samuel was not afraid. When we want something so strongly, many times our desire will override our fear.

BE SUBMITTED

The instructions Eli gave to Samuel concerning hearing God's voice are so simple that it is easy to overlook some very important aspects contained in them. He advised Samuel to ask the "**Lord**" to speak to him. This would acknowledge Samuel's submitted relationship to God. He is the submitted servant and God is ruler over his life. A submitted servant stands in readiness to do the bidding of his lord and master. At one time the children of Israel stated, "*All that the Lord has spoken we will do*" (Exodus 19:8). However, God, knowing the hidden issues of their heart, said "*Oh, that they had such a heart in them that they would fear Me and always keep My commandments*" (Deuteronomy 5:29).

To hear the word of the Lord is to be faced with the choice of responding in obedience. Some of the leaders during the time Ezekiel prophesied had a different mindset. They would come to Ezekiel because they knew God would speak to him. Sometimes it even seemed like they enjoyed hearing Ezekiel speak, but God discerned their true motives. He told Ezekiel that they were listening to the word in the same way they would listen to a beautiful piece of music. God's words were pleasant to hear, but they had no intention of following through in obedience.

HAVE A LISTENING EAR

The Psalmist said in Psalm 85:8, "*I will hear what God the Lord will speak.*" Eli admonished Samuel to respond to God with these words, "*Your servant is listening.*" Perhaps this was said to teach Samuel responsible behavior when God spoke. Most of us are poor listeners. If we are not interrupting each other or talking at the same, we are distracted by our own thought life. Even our quiet times with the Lord have become quite noisy as we present Him with our long list of requests. After we have told Him what we want, how and when we want it, we consider our prayer time ended. God never intended to have one-sided communication with us. We are to listen so that we can hear His response. The next chapter will expand further on the importance of having a listening ear.

SUMMARY

We looked at a model for learning to hear the voice of God based on the instructions Eli gave to Samuel. Learning to hear involves taking an initial step. It also means that we must come to a place of rest. Asking God to speak, being expectant to hear, and having a listening ear were additional parts of our model. And lastly, the importance of being submitted and responsive to God undergirds this model.

PRAYER

Lord, I invite you to speak to me. I am listening. Amen.

PAUSE AND REFLECT

Consider the role that Eli had in Samuel's life as a mentor. What were some of the elements involved in their relationship? Do you have someone who has served a similar role in your life?

Tell how Samuel's experience may have turned out if Eli had not been there to guide him.

Identify the steps included in the instruction Eli gave to Samuel for hearing the voice of God.

Which of these steps do you need to start working on now?

Which of these steps have been difficult for you to implement in the past?

How do you plan to use the information shared in this section?

What has God spoken to you through this chapter? Write it here.

QUIET TIME: BE STILL AND KNOW

Speak, Lord. Your servant is listening. What is He saying? Write it here.

CHAPTER 6

Focused Listening

"Listen to Me, you who follow after righteousness you who seek the Lord, listen to Me My people and give ear to Me. O My nation, listen to me. You people who know righteousness; you people in whose heart is My law" Isaiah 51:7

We serve a talking God and in order to hear what He has to say we need to have ears to hear. Jesus would sometimes preface a particularly important point with the words, *"He that has ears to hear, let him hear"* (Matthew 11:15; 13:9; Mark 4:9; 4:23; 7:16; Luke 8:18).

To improve communication skills, experts in the field of psychology and communication have stressed the importance of attentive or active listening. Active listening is when you make a conscious effort to go beyond just hearing the words another person is saying to you. An important element of active listening is that you are able to hear the complete message that is being given to you. This means you must pay very close attention to the other person.

Before there were communication experts such as we know today, God gave Ezekiel a lesson on focused listening. God spoke to him as he was entering a new phase in his prophetic ministry. Ezekiel was going to receive visions and revelations of a new temple. God was also giving him prophetic words to speak to the children of Israel during their captivity. Apparently, God didn't want Ezekiel to miss any aspect of what He had to say. Therefore, He gave him these instructions, *"Son of man, look with your eyes, and hear with your ears, and fix your mind on everything I show you"* (Ezekiel 40:4).

Eyes. Ears. Mind. Focused listening requires bringing all these faculties to attention. As attentive listeners, we enter the presence of God and focus on Him to experience who He is and all that He is. We are to meditate on the *"I AM THAT I AM"* who wants to speak to and with us (Exodus 3:4). In Revelation 1:9-17, John gives a beautiful detailed description of Jesus. His description shows that he focused on the majesty of the One before him. Jesus had his complete attention.

BEWARE OF DISTRACTIONS

When we are focused listeners it means that we have learned to free ourselves from distractions. Distractions are things that cause us to turn away from the original focus of attention or interest. Recently a young woman shared a dream in which she was being bitten by mosquitoes. She said she kept slapping her arms and legs, which eventually became quite sore. She said when she prayed about the dream, she felt the Lord spoke to her and said, "You are distracted by the distractions."

"Distracted by the distractions!" That's what happened to Peter when Jesus took him, along with James and John, to the Mount of Transfiguration (Matthew 17:1-13). The appearance of the super saints Moses and Elijah proved to be a distraction for Peter. Their presence sent him into some sort of mental reverie wherein he envisioned himself constructing tabernacles. God had to caution him and encourage him to stay focused. There is no indication that Peter's companions were similarly distracted. John often referred to himself as the disciple that Jesus loved. He is portrayed as leaning on Jesus' breast. John had learned to stay focused by positioning himself so that he could hear even the whispers that came from the Savior's lips.

POISED TO LISTEN

Habakkuk 2:1 NIV says, *"I will stand upon my watch and set me upon the tower, and will look forth to see what He will speak with me, and what I shall answer concerning my complaint."* The prophets were compared to watchmen positioned in a tower who were diligent in watching out for the welfare of the people. The tower was a fenced-in place. It was narrow and tight so that the one occupying it seemed to be hemmed in. Upon the tower the prophet watched patiently and constantly to catch the first approach of an unexpected visitor, but also to hear the voice of the Lord. Symbolically, entering the tower means the prophet is moving to a higher level of increased vision. He is moving to a place of freedom from distractions so that he can hear the voice of God clearly.

Habakkuk was committed to "stand upon his watch." Sometimes there is a period of waiting before God speaks. Impatience and anxiety often pulls us out of God's presence before He has a chance to speak to us. Several years ago, Christians held meetings called "shut ins." They would go to the church or at someone's home for overnight or several days and engage in focused prayer and intercession. It was a corporate gathering for seeking the Lord and waiting to hear what He had to say. The period of prayer was always accompanied with fasting. No one would leave the building until the shut in was over.

The shut in reflected a period of coming away from worldly distractions and turning the eyes, ears and heart upward toward heaven. It was very common to hear many of the participants say, "I need to hear from God." This desire to hear from God was so intense that it pulled the seekers into His presence where they could give full attention to waiting on Him. Habakkuk purposed in his heart to stay in the watchtower (his Hearing Position) where he knew God would speak to him.

He said he would, *"look forth to see what God would speak"* to him. This indicates a state of expectancy. He had positioned himself to watch for the word of the Lord to come to his heart. As a watchman, he is vigilant and stands on guard to be ready to receive the word of the Lord when it comes. He must not fall asleep or get caught up in the sights and sounds of his environment. He is a soldier at full attention. To him the voice of God is such a reality that he seems to describe it as something tangible. He *"looks forth to see"* what God will say and he knows the word of the Lord will come to his listening ear.

STAYING FOCUSED

Another biblical example of a focused listener is Mary, the sister of Martha and Lazarus. We are introduced to her in Luke 10:39 and told that she "*sat at Jesus' feet and heard His word.*" When Jesus came to their house to share a meal there were many things that were potential sources of distraction. She had to deal with her sister's frustrations regarding her lack of participation in the food preparation. Martha's attitude could have been a distraction. Martha expected Mary to perform in a certain way. We can be thrown off course or moved from our original focus by the expectations of others. There are times when we go to great efforts to avoid conflict even when it means we are moved from His presence.

Even the noise of Martha's meal preparation intruded upon Mary's time with the Lord to lure her away. Remember how we were as kids? When our parents would get on the telephone we would start making noise to direct their attention to us? Can you also recall being in school at a basketball game? When a member of the opposing team would be ready to shoot the ball, you would yell or do something to try to break their concentration. A focused listener must learn to tune out the noise.

As we pray and ask God to uncover the sources of noise in our lives, He will reveal them to us. Jesus told Martha that she was "*cumbered about much serving.*" Cumbered is like our word distracted. The Lord was telling Martha that the tasks of serving were drawing her away from Him. This is not necessarily a negative comment about Martha. It can be interpreted as an expression of Jesus' desire to be with her.

Martha had become distracted by what seemed to her necessary tasks. Yes, if you invite a person to dinner they must be fed. But was dinner the original priority, or was it, "Lord, I'd really love to spend some time with you? Please come by. Don't worry about dinner. I'll fix something." Somehow for Martha things got reversed and now the meal is the main order of the day. We are like that, aren't we? We spend so much time on the details, the things that God has identified as less important. Hearing from God requires us to re-order our priorities. That is the message He lovingly gave to Martha.

In reference to Mary, Jesus said, "She made a good choice." Probably both of the sisters had been anxiously awaiting and anticipating the arrival of their friend. Martha would show off her culinary skills and Mary would just hang around Him. When He came, Mary positioned herself at His feet. She wanted to be so close to Him as to ward off all distractions. Perhaps it wasn't easy for Mary to become an attentive listener, because as Martha pointed out to Jesus there were other things that needed to be done. Yet it seems she had disciplined herself to become a focused listener. Even being misunderstood was not enough to remove her attention from Jesus.

Our Lord loves it when we give Him this kind of attention. On earth, we are learning to respond to Him as He is responded to in heaven. In heaven, all eyes are upon Him. All attention goes to Him. He is worshipped day and night. There is no place for distractions in heaven.

SUMMARY

We all have to deal with the distractions that cause us to be less attentive to spiritual things. To hear the voice of God clearly, we are required to practice focused listening. Focused listening means that our eyes, ears and thoughts are tuned into Him.

PRAYER

Jesus, help me to pay attention! Amen!

PAUSE AND REFLECT

When it comes to your quiet time, what do you see as the biggest distraction in your life right now?

Do you have a plan for dealing with distractions which occur during your quiet time?

Tell what you like about Martha. Tell what you like about Mary.

Are you a Mary or a Martha?

What keeps you focused on your pursuit of God?

What has God spoken to you through this chapter? Write it here.

Tell how you will use the information in this chapter to help you stay focused. Be specific.

QUIET TIME: BE STILL AND KNOW

See yourself sitting at the feet of Jesus now. What is He saying? Write it here.

CHAPTER 7

My Sheep Hear My Voice

"I am the good shepherd. The good shepherd gives His life for His sheep... My sheep hear My voice and I know them, and they follow Me." John10:11, 27

We serve a talking God. He has made us talking people. He created us in His own image thereby giving us the ability to communicate with Him. This talking God has something to say and He wants to say it to us. He wants us to be able to hear His voice and to recognize when He speaks to us.

Giving audience to God is essential in knowing His will for our lives. If we will give God our attention, we will hear His voice and receive direction from Him.

THE GOOD SHEPHERD

The tenth chapter of John contains the parable of the Good Shepherd. This parable is about the interaction of a shepherd with his sheep. It offers insight into the process of how God interacts with us to teach us to hear His voice. After sharing the qualities that are present in a caring shepherd Jesus states plainly, *"I am the good shepherd"* (v.11). What is the good shepherd like and how do those characteristics enhance our ability to hear? This question will be answered by looking at the verses in John 10:1-30. (Reading this now is recommended).

A SHEPHERD WE CAN HEAR

In John 10:3, Jesus said, *"The sheep hear His voice: and He calls his own sheep by name, and leads them out."* From this we can see that sheep can hear the voice of the shepherd. The reason they can hear is because they were created with a pair of ears. This is a simple and obvious fact, isn't it? But we must start with this fact because we often think we must be uniquely equipped spiritually before we can hear God. It is good to remember God has given us everything we need. Jesus confirms this in Matthew 11:15 when He said, *"He who has ears to hear let him hear."* To paraphrase this verse, "If you want to hear, use the basic equipment that I (Jesus) have given to you."

We have not only been given spiritual ears, but ears that have been specially prepared to hear. Psalm 40:6 states, *"My ears you have opened."* The word "opened" means to dig out. God has dug out our ears as one would dig a well. Our ears have been opened so that they can receive communication of truth. Isaiah 50:5 echoes this where the Messiah speaks saying, *"The Lord God has opened my ear."* Just think about this wonderful truth! Our spiritual ears have been opened for the express purpose of hearing the voice of God. You have ears to hear!

A SHEPHERD UP CLOSE AND PERSONAL

The sheep's identity and perception of who they are is connected to what they hear from the shepherd. The shepherd calls the sheep and speaks to them individually. Anyone who has observed a shepherd interact with his sheep will tell you that his communication with each sheep is very personal.

The shepherd gives each sheep a name. Often these names are based on the sheep's physical appearance. They may be given names such as Short Legs, Big Ears or Bright Eyes. A name can also be based on their behavioral characteristics and a sheep could be called Courageous, Stubborn, Leader or Strong Boy. Aren't you glad that we are not some "Hey You!" with God? Nathaniel asked Jesus, *"How do you know me?"* (John 1:48). His question gives expression to the same feeling of awe inside us when we suddenly realize that in the midst of all the people on planet earth, God knows *my* name.

The shepherd calls the sheep by name. By naming them He assures Himself of a way to get the sheep's attention. He will use their name repeatedly when talking to them. Thus, the more the shepherd speaks to them, the more accustomed to his voice they become. This was illustrated in the story of Samuel.

A SHEPHERD WHO INITIATES

The shepherd is the initiator in the communication. He does not wait for the sheep to speak to him first. When Jesus would see a person He wanted for a disciple, He would go up to that person and start a conversation. It would not necessarily be a long dialogue. As a matter of fact, it was often just a few words such as, *"Follow Me."* For an example, look at the case of two pairs of brothers as told in Matthew 4:18-22.

We meet Andrew and Peter first. It seems they were just starting to work when Jesus passed by where they were fishing. He walked up to them and told them to follow Him and He would change their job description. Instead of catching fish, they would be soul winners. Then, Jesus, with Andrew and Peter now following Him, walked further down the seashore and spotted two more brothers. He invited James and John to follow Him. In both instances, Jesus was the initiator of the first contact. God will take the lead in teaching us how to hear His voice. Calvary testifies to the extent God goes to initiate communication with us.

A SHEPHERD WE CAN FOLLOW

The shepherd goes ahead of the sheep and shows them the way they are to go. He guides them with the sound of his voice. As Christians, we want God to lead us right into the center of His will. Even if we know where we want to go, we often don't know how to get there. Jeremiah said, "*O, Lord, I know the way of man is not in himself. It is not in man who walks to direct his own steps*" (Jeremiah 10:23). David said in Psalm 23:2, "*He leads me beside the still waters*," and in 23:3, "*He leads me in the paths of righteousness, for His name's sake.*"

God always leads us in the route that takes us back to Him. We don't have to worry and fear that we will end up in some strange out of the way place on the edge of nowhere without Him. Neither will He, as a faithful shepherd, lead us down self-destructive paths. The story is told of a man who observed another man who was behind some sheep attempting to drive them into a pen. He asked someone who stood by why the shepherd was herding the sheep in that manner. The reply came back quickly. "My friend, that is not the shepherd. That man is the butcher."

A SHEPHERD WE CAN KNOW

The Shepherd brings out his own sheep and goes before them and the sheep follow him because they have come to know his voice. There is a progression here. First the sheep hear his voice, and then they know his voice. There are different kinds of knowing and different degrees of knowing. Let's look at "yada", one of the Hebrew words for knowing. This word is rich with shadings and depth of meaning.

"Yada" means to be acquainted with a person. In Job 22:21, his friend Eliphaz tells him to become acquainted with God. While this may convey to us the idea of the first stage of a relationship, it means something more. It contains the idea of becoming familiar with a person through service to them. Eliphaz's instruction to Job is to become a servant to God. In this sense yada is knowledge that is gained as the result of having a servant relationship with a person. Knowing God is related to having a servant's heart.

And what is a servant's heart? It is simply an attitude of obedience to carry out the Master's commands. Perhaps it is best summed up in the words of Mary, the mother of Jesus, at the marriage celebration in Cana (see John 2:1-11). A crisis arose due to a shortage of wine. Mary, confident that Jesus would resolve the crisis in some way, went to the servants and told them, *"Whatever He says to you, do it"* (v.5).

Yada can infer intimacy in relationships, hence deeper levels of knowing. Consider Deuteronomy 34: 10 which addresses Moses' relationship with God. Moses communed with God face-to-face. The words of God's mouth could flow unhindered to Moses because Moses continually walked in the direction of God. *"Let him kiss me with the kisses of his mouth"* is the plea from the Shulamite in Song of Solomon 1:2. God's words to us are as kisses placed tenderly and strategically upon our mouth. The deepest knowledge of God is contained in His word. Jesus said we are to search the Scriptures because they speak about Him.

We experience yada at this level as we walk in an attitude of obedience and set our heart to know God's heart. We are told that David was after God's heart. He wanted to understand what was in God's heart and the quest for knowing God became a passionate pursuit.

At its deepest level yada relates to sexual intimacy. Perhaps as a kid you would wonder how a husband in the Bible could know his wife (as in *"Adam knew his wife Eve"*) and she ended up having a baby. Well that kind of knowing as in Adam knowing Eve is about sexual intercourse. From a spiritual perspective, sexual intimacy is all about surrender. As we yield ourselves totally to God we become spiritual containers into which He can pour fountains of revelation about who He is.

A SHEPHERD WE CAN FULLY KNOW

God wants us to fully know Him. Listen to the words of the Psalmist in 139:1-6, *"O Lord, You have searched me and **known** me. You **know** my sitting down and my rising up: You **understand** my thought afar off. You **comprehend** my path and lying down, and are **acquainted** with all my ways, for there is not a word on my tongue, but behold, O Lord, You **know** it altogether. You have hedged me behind and before, and laid Your hand on me. Such **knowledge** is too wonderful for me; it is high, I cannot attain it"* (Emphasis added).

The Psalmist is aware of how complete God's knowledge is of him. He describes God as someone who has conducted an intimate search of him. God knows about the daily routine of his life, his thoughts, the direction his life takes, even the desires that will come to him in the future. The Psalmist is blown away by this knowledge. He is overwhelmed and overcome with awe and amazement.

It is possible for us to yada God in this way also. God wants us to know His voice because it is the way by which we get to know Him. Our goal is to fully know His voice with all its tones and intonations, points of emphasis, wording, volume, etc. The more we hear His voice, the more fully we will know His voice. The more fully we know His voice, the more we will be able to receive direction and guidance from Him so that we can walk in complete obedience.

SUMMARY

Jesus is the Good Shepherd who has equipped His sheep with the ability to hear. A shepherd names his sheep to establish the sheep's identity. Our Good Shepherd knows our name and uses this name when He speaks to us. He takes the initiative in teaching us to hear and we learn to trust Him and to follow Him.

PRAYER

May I know God in the same measure that He knows me. Amen.

PAUSE AND REFLECT

Read Psalm 23. How do you think this Psalm relates to hearing the voice of God?

What is God's purpose in leading us by still waters?

Psalm 23 addresses the issues of fear and anxiety. How does fear and anxiety interfere with hearing?

Tell how trust is a necessary component in learning to hear the voice of God.

How will the concept of Jesus as the Good Shepherd aid you in your quest to know the voice of God?

What has God spoken to you through this chapter? Write it here.

Tell how you will apply the teachings in this chapter in your life this week.

QUIET TIME: BE STILL AND KNOW

The Good Shepherd calls you by a new name. What is it? What does it mean? Write it here.

SPEAK LORD WORKSHEET

Refer to the last "Speak Lord Worksheet" that you completed. Has God spoken to you about the situation you described? If so, you may either skip this page or write about another concern.

1. One thing that I would like for God to speak to me about is:

2. This is what I feel that God has already spoken to me regarding my concern:

3. It is important for God to speak to me about this area of my life because:

4. This is what I will do in response to what God tells me:

CHAPTER 8

Competing Voices

"And when He brings out His own sheep, He goes before them, and the sheep follow Him, for they know His voice. Yet they will by no means follow a stranger, for they do not know the voice of strangers."
John 10:4,5

We serve a talking God who loves us so much that He wants to communicate that love to us. He has given us the ability to communicate with Him, and He takes the lead in getting the dialogue started.

When the Creator and the created can converse with each other, we have one of the most powerful communication networks in the universe. For this very reason, we would expect to encounter some attempt to run interference with it. And that is exactly what happened.

Let's take another look at the parable of the good shepherd. John 10:5 states, *"Yet they will by no means follow a stranger, but will flee from him for they know not the voice of strangers."* From this we see that in addition to the shepherd's voice, the sheep must now deal with the voice of strangers. Strangers are foreign elements or the static in our hearing equation. They represent the other voices competing for our attention.

OTHER VOICES

When we are open to spiritual things, there are other strange voices that attempt to broadcast over our airwaves. Some of these voices are subtle so we must learn to identify them. In 1 John 4:1 we read, *"Beloved, believe not every spirit, but test the spirits to see whether they are of God because many false prophets have gone out into the world."*

In learning to hear from God we are faced with this age-old problem, discerning the voice of God from other voices. This problem first surfaced in the Garden of Eden. There, we were introduced to the concept of competing voices. These voices can be narrowed down to just three. They are the voice of God, the voice of Adam and Eve, which we will refer to as the voice of self and the voice of the serpent, which we will refer to as the voice of the enemy. Each of these voices will be discussed briefly in the section that follows and will be explored in greater detail in subsequent chapters.

THE VOICE OF THE ENEMY

When the serpent approached Eve, his goal for communicating with her became readily apparent. His strategy was to cast doubt on her ability to hear clearly from God. He initiated conversation with Eve by asking the question, *"Now has God indeed said, 'you shall not eat of every tree of the garden'?"* (Genesis 3:1) *"Has God indeed said?"* Isn't that basically our struggle in hearing from God, trying to answer that question. "Is this God, self or the enemy?" These are the most important voices in our own life, which we are expected to discern. When we discern something, we render a judgment about it. We are asking, "Is the voice I hear God or not God?" We could render a judgment by saying, "This is indeed the voice of God to me" or "No, this isn't God's voice".

The serpent's question to Eve was designed and intended to do more than just cast doubt on her ability to hear the voice of God. He also wanted her to question her ability to interpret accurately what God had spoken to her. However, the real motive behind the enemy's voice was to assassinate the character of God. If God is now perceived as withholding, controlling and self -serving, rather than lovloving, generous and kind, then there is no benefit to be experienced in listening to His voice and obeying Him.

By heeding to the voice of the enemy, Eve was assenting to his mischaracterization of God. We must always validate God's character and essence and not be confused by things that seemingly cast doubt on the goodness of God. Life's challenges and difficulties can cause us to question the fairness of things. Yet, we must continue to affirm the inherent goodness of God even in the face of life's severest tests and trials. We are to come into agreement with the Psalmist who reminds us that God's goodness and mercy endure forever (Psalm 136).

Since Adam and Eve had only been exposed to the voice of God and the sound of their own voices, it seems they would have recognized the voice of the enemy. Perhaps they did recognize it as a stranger's voice, but were not skillful in discerning the stranger's true character. The enemy was successful in reaching his goal, and the nature of communication between God and Adam and Eve changed. After that, when God came to commune with them, the sound of His voice evoked a fear response (Genesis 3:8-11). Adam told God that when he heard His approach he became afraid. That fear caused Adam to run away from God and hide. Sadly, God's presence was no longer experienced as inviting and comforting. It became something from which to shrink away.

The excuse that Adam gave to God for hiding from Him was that he was afraid because he was naked. Please note that God and Adam are still communicating, but it is not in the same way. His communication with God is filled with guilt, excuses and blaming. Adam and Eve even blamed God for some of their problems. They were not seeing or hearing clearly any more. The enemy's attack was so subtle they didn't even see what hit them.

THE VOICE OF GOD

God spoke to Adam to help him discern the voice of the enemy. First, he called Adam by name. Adam was hiding and God wanted to bring him back into His presence. When we are in God's presence, as in walking in obedience to Him, we are more open and sensitive to His voice. When we are out of His presence, as in walking in our own way, He will call us back through the conviction of Holy Spirit.

Next, He asked Adam, "*Where are you?*" Did God know where Adam was? Of course He did! However, it was only after God asked the question that Adam identified himself as being in a place of hiding. The question not only helped Adam to identify where he was, it also brought him back into dialogue with God.

Then, God asked Adam, "*Who told you that you were naked?*" In other words, "Adam, whose voice have you been listening to? I did not tell you that. In fact, I would not have told you that because it would have been a lie. When I created you, you were pure and innocent and there was no shame or nakedness due to sin. So, where did you get this information?"

God wanted them to know His voice and He did not sever His relationship with them. Instead, He engaged Adam in further dialogue by asking him if he had eaten from the tree that had been off limits for them. His questioning was designed to help Adam become aware of one of the basic obstacles to hearing the voice of God, which was his disobedience.

THE VOICE OF MAN

Eve acknowledged that the serpent had deceived her. When we are deceived, we are led astray. We must ask, "What made Eve vulnerable to being led astray?" The answer may lie in her desire to live independently of God. Apparently, she decided she didn't need to receive from Him the wisdom that would structure her life. She desired wisdom to flow from her own mouth and not the mouth of God. However, Jesus said, "*It is written, "man shall not live by bread alone, but by every word that proceeds out of the mouth of God'"*(Matthew 4:4).

Christians are called to live by God's word. If we order our lives by His words, we will not have to rely on our own wits to see us through various circumstances. Jacob lived by his wits, directing his life by his own voice. God kept speaking to him through dreams and visions and life circumstances. Thus, Jacob gradually moved from his wisdom as the guiding force in his life to God's wisdom.

We, like Eve, can be led astray when we forget that God is the source of our wisdom. In 1 Corinthians 1:30, we read, *"But of Him you are in Christ Jesus, who became for us wisdom from God, and righteousness, and sanctification and redemption."* God wants to be a continual source of wisdom to guide and direct us in the way that we should go.

The communication network that was torn down between God and Adam and Eve seems to have been restored. When their first son, Cain, was born Eve said, *"I have acquired a man from the Lord"* (Genesis 4:1). God is faithful to restore that which was torn down even to the extent of sending His only Son to Earth to communicate accurately His nature and character.

TELEVISION CHANNELS

A useful metaphor for enhancing your understanding of competing voices would be the idea of channels on a television. Each channel gives us a specific type of programming. If we tune into a channel with a program that we don't want to watch, we can switch the channel. We also have the advantage of using a remote control, which makes the channel switching easier. The word of God is the remote control in our life. At the instant, we tune into something other than God-inspired wisdom, Holy Spirit will let us know that we need to switch the channel. We can then use the remote control by meditating on God's word.

SUMMARY

If Adam and Eve had not been tempted in the Garden of Eden, we probably would not have to deal with the concept of competing voices. Unfortunately, that is not the case and we must learn to discern between the voice of God, our own voice, and the voice of the enemy. God wants to control the spiritual airways related to communicating with Him.

PRAYER

Lord, help me to recognize my own voice and discern the voice of the enemy. Let my airways be clear, so that You can speak to me. Help me switch channels as soon as I become aware that I have tuned into the wrong voice. Amen.

PAUSE AND REFLECT

Describe the concept of competing voices.

Which of the three voices is easiest for you to discern?

Which of the three voices is the most difficult to discern?

How will you use the concept of the remote control to help you switch the channel?

Analyze the dialogue between Eve and the serpent. Where did she have opportunities to switch the channel?

Does the voice of the enemy ever come to you in a way that mischaracterizes God? For example, are you ever tempted to doubt God's love or faithfulness to you?

What do you need to remember about God's character today?

Give examples of how you will apply the teachings from this lesson.

What has God spoken to you through this chapter? Write it here.

<u>QUIET TIME: BE STILL AND KNOW</u>

God speaks to you something about His character. What is it? Write it here.

CHAPTER 9

General Principles of Discernment

"Your ears shall hear a word behind you, saying, 'This is the way, walk in it,' whenever you turn to the right hand or whenever you turn to the left." Isaiah 30:21

We serve a talking God. He wants us to be able to discern His voice from all the other voices that vie for our attention. In this section, we will take a closer look at the meaning of discernment.

WHAT IS DISCERNMENT

There are several words in the Greek relating to discernment that will help us arrive at a definition. We will look at two of these. The first word is "diakrisis" which is translated discern in Hebrews 5:14, *"But solid food belongs to those who are of full age, that is, those who by reason of use have their senses exercised to discern both good and evil..."* and 1 Corinthians 12:10, *"to another the working of miracles, to another prophecy, to another discerning of spirits, to another different kinds of tongues, to another the interpretation of tongues"*. In these verses discern means to know the difference between good and evil and attaining knowledge that leads us to Christ. Simply stated, it is the ability to decide between truth and error.

In 1 Thessalonians 5:21 Paul says, *"Test all things. Hold fast what is good."* Here the Greek word for "test" is "dokimazo". It means to test, examine, prove and scrutinize to see whether a thing is genuine or not. It refers to a test applied to metals or as we would ask, "Is it the genuine article?" Thus, dokimazo also infers that some conclusion is drawn. It means to recognize as genuine after examination and to approve or deem worthy. Discernment, then, is that ability which helps us to make decisions regarding the inherent quality of something.

Like Samuel, we initially learn to discern by trial and error. However, there are some conditions that aid us in this process. We will discuss a few of these.

DESIRE TO FOLLOW JESUS

Jesus said, "*My sheep... follow me*" (John 10:27). We must desire to follow Him and desire to do His will. Desire is the first requirement. We will define desire as "earnestly wanting". Related to this is the idea of being open to God. We are to be willing for Him to teach us what He wants us to know. We sometimes get locked into our own agenda and start writing our lesson plans. One of the disciples was so caught up in what was going to happen to a fellow disciple that He almost missed what Jesus wanted to say to Him. Jesus had to tell him to stop worrying about the other person and to keep his eyes on Him (John 21:19-22). In other words, Jesus was trying to get the disciple to drop his agenda and to tune into His.

When we ask God to help us to discern His voice because we want to know His will, we do not always know what the outcome will be. Therefore, a desire to follow Him relates to taking the road He lays out before us. His word, which is His voice to us, becomes the lamp that guides our feet (Psalm 119:105). If we set preconditions on obeying Him, we may not be able to hear His voice clearly. Some of the kings in the Old Testament would ask for a prophet to tell them God's will. But when it was not what they wanted to hear, they would call the prophet a false prophet. They were clearly fixed in their agenda and failed to discern that God was truly speaking.

PRAYER

Next, we are to be given to prayer. Prayer and waiting on God are essential to the hearing process. Prayer calls us to attention and puts in a frame of mind to hear. Waiting in the presence of the Lord gives us the opportunity to hear. Prayer is a process of waiting, listening, pondering and responding.

Spending time in prayer communicates to God our desire to hear. If we say we want to hear and yet fail to spend time with God, our behavior cancels out our words. When we draw near to God, He responds by drawing near to us.

KNOW THE WORD

Knowing what the Bible says is important. This point has been emphasized again and again throughout this book. The Bible is God's voice to us and teaches us what He sees as essential for us to know. The Bible is our tester. Everything we hear must line up with the Bible, the written word of God. Ignorance of the Scriptures can leave us open to unnecessary confusion. Knowledge of the Bible will bring clarity to anything you feel God has spoken to you.

OBEY

The Christian who wants to hear from God should cultivate the practice of walking in obedience to Him. This also includes being submissive and responsive to the spiritual leaders that God has placed in your life. Hebrews 13:17 admonishes, *"Obey them that have the rule over you, and submit to them: for they watch in behalf of your souls, as they that shall give account; that they may do this with joy, and not with grief: for that would be unprofitable for you."* Spiritual accountability helps to protect us from some Hearing Errors.

CONFESSION OF SIN

We are not perfect, but continually strive toward maturity in our Christian walk. Occasionally we may sin or make mistakes. When this occurs, we need to be quick to repent. If we procrastinate in this area, whether due to guilt, condemnation or hardness of heart, it is like plugging up our spiritual ears. Sin is like earwax in our ears. The more it builds up, the less keen our hearing becomes. Let's get rid of the earwax by having the humility of a repentant heart. Remember, *"If we confess our sins, He is faithful and just to forgive us our sins and to cleanse us from all unrighteousness"* (1 John. 1:9).

SEEK COUNSEL

Proverbs 11:14 says, *"Where there is no counsel, the people fall; but in the multitude of counselors there is safety."* God will place godly men and women in your life who can mentor you in your ability to discern. When you are confused or just unsure about the source of the voice speaking to you, ask for their counsel. I have found that this is a safety valve for me. Even if I am sure about something, there are times when I will still submit it to others with whom I have spiritual accountability. I have found that when I am too sure about a thing, I am in fact too sure.

KNOW GOD

Finally, but perhaps the most important condition of all, is to know what God is like. This will be addressed in more detail in the chapter on *Discerning the Voice of the Enemy* but it is relevant to this section also. As we have seen, Adam and Eve missed it here. The serpent came and cast doubt on the character of God and Eve lacked intimate knowledge of God. Not once did she reflect and say, "NO! You are a liar! God is not like that!"

SUMMARY

While learning to know the voice of God, one of the tasks we encounter is being able to discern God's voice from other voices. We labeled these competing voices as the voice of the self and the voice of the enemy. Several things were discussed that serve as aids in helping us to discern what voice is speaking to us. It was concluded that probably the most important safe guard of all is to know what God is like.

PRAYER

Father, teach me to be able to discern Your voice. Amen.

PAUSE AND REFLECT

Write out your definition of discern. Use Scripture to help you clarify your definition.

List the principles of discernment discussed in this chapter.

Which principles are you currently putting into practice?

Which principles do you need to start observing now?

Do you have accountability relationships? If so, how have they aided you in the process of discernment?

If you do not have an accountability relationship, is there someone you trust enough to ask them to serve this role in your life?

Share one way that you will make use of the principles of discernment.

What has God spoken to you through this chapter? Write it here.

QUIET TIME: BE STILL AND KNOW

God validates you. What is He saying? Write it here.

CHAPTER 10

Discerning the Voice of the Flesh (Part 1)

*"There is a way that seems right to a man,
but its end is the way of death." Proverbs 14:12*

We serve a talking God. There are other voices that compete with the voice of God, so we must learn to discern between them. The voices that we are interested in discerning are our own voice (or the voice of the flesh or self), the voice of the enemy, and the voice of God.

THE VOICE OF THE FLESH

The voice of the flesh is simply our own thoughts. There are several variations on the term thought as used in the Hebrew language but it is most often used to convey the idea of planning or devising. Joseph used this word when he told his brothers *"But as for you, you meant* (devised or planned) *evil against me"* (Genesis 50:20). Two additional examples will give further clarity to this term. Genesis 6:5 states, *"The Lord saw that the wickedness of man was great in the earth, and every intent of the thoughts of his heart was only evil continually."* Then in Jeremiah 18:12, the children of Israel spoke in rebellion against God and said, *"That is hopeless! So we will walk according to our own plans, and we will every one obey the dictates of his own evil heart."*

The above references shed light on Isaiah 55:8-9 where God says, *"For My thoughts are not your thoughts, nor are your ways My ways, says the Lord. For as the heavens are high above the earth, so are My ways higher than your ways, and My thoughts than your thoughts."* Herein is a word of caution; we are to make a distinction between our thoughts and God's thoughts. We are not to assume that everything that pops into our heads is God speaking to us. We always have the ability to think our own thoughts. If a person does not possess this ability, then we say that person is "brainwashed'.

Some of our thoughts are considered good by our own standards. However, a good thing must be differentiated from a God thing. Uzzah thought it was a good thing to reach out his hand and steady the Ark of the Covenant. It was a good thought, but God wasn't in it and the consequences for him were fatal (2 Samuel 6:1-6).

We can also look at a situation in the life of David. He was entering the declining years of his ministry and hadn't realized his dream of building a temple. He ran the idea by Nathan, the prophet, who encouraged him to do all that was in his heart. Later, God corrected Nathan and he went back to David and told him that God was not in that plan. We could say, "Oh, what a marvelous, unselfish, generous thought David had!" Even God acknowledged to David that his desire to build the temple was delightful and pleasing to Him, but He did not bless that desire. It was still a David thought and not a God thought.

In each of these examples there wasn't anything evil or sinister in what they wanted to do that would cause us to ascribe their behavior to the influence of the enemy. They all had good thoughts, but they were thoughts that originated from their own heart's desire. For more examples of self-thoughts see Luke 16:3 & 18:4.

WE HAVE A VOICE

Therefore, we need to know the sound of our own voice. What does your voice sound like? Have you ever talked to yourself? Of course, you have. We do this a lot. In fact, we do it so much we don't even recognize we're doing it. Occasionally we may slip and say something out loud, but for the most part these are just inner thoughts. Most of them do not even get shared with anyone.

The voice of self is rooted in the all- about- me things of our life. This includes our background, culture, education and social status. These are the things that control what we hear and how we interpret what we hear. Even the apostle Paul said he had to die to the influence of these things (Philippians 3:4-9). The thoughts of our heart include imaginations, plans, desires and devices which are to be submitted to the word of God and prayer.

Jeremiah 3:17 says, *"At that time Jerusalem shall be called 'the Throne of the Lord', and all nations shall be gathered to it. No more shall they follow the dictates of their evil hearts."* When God spoke of establishing His throne, He was declaring a prophetic promise to the children of Israel because at that time, He was not ruling in their hearts. In fact, it was the exact opposite! Self was enthroned. Self seeks to fulfill its own desires. When not surrendered to Holy Spirit it will accomplish its own ends. Eve's thought life was influenced by the enemy, but also by self -motivation. The thought in her heart was to be like God and she wanted to be equal with Him in knowledge. She was prideful in her heart and pride is one of the things that gives a voice to the flesh.

RECOGNIZING THE VOICE OF THE FLESH

Separating out our voice from the other voices is often the most difficult of the three. One of the reasons for this is that we fail to discern our own heart. How much do we know about the secret places of our heart? Secret places are not necessarily places of deception. They are most likely things that are out of our awareness. Simon Peter certainly is a comforting example of one who, like us, misjudged what was in his heart. Jesus told him that He would deny Him three times. Peter protested vehemently that it would never happen. He insisted on his readiness to lay down his life for Christ. And, yes, he probably actually believed it at the time he spoke. However, the penetrating eyes of Jesus went into the hidden areas of his heart and brought to the surface what Peter had not discerned (Matthew 26:31 -35).

David prayed, *"Who can understand his errors? Cleanse me from secret faults"* (Psalm 19:12). Just how are we cleansed from the secret faults? To answer that, we turn again to the writings of David. David makes a bold and courageous request of God. He prays, *"Search me O God and know my heart; try me and know my anxieties; and see if there is any wicked way in me and lead me into life everlasting"* (Psalm 139:23-24). David's prayer has been made into a beautiful song, but have we really meditated on the power of his words? He prays for God to search his heart. If our heart had layers, David has given God permission to go to the deepest layer.

A MODEL TO HELP DISCERN

In the field of psychology there is something called the Jo-Hari window, which was developed, by Harry Luft and Joseph Ingham. The Jo-Hari window is a model of awareness providing for feedback and disclosure. It has been used in a variety of settings, especially in the work place to look at interpersonal relationships. Here is a simplified explanation of the model.

The basic concept of the Jo-Hari window relates to self-awareness. There are some things that I know about me, that you also know. These things, which we both know, make that area of my life "Known". There are some things about me that I know, but you don't know. The things that I know, but you don't, are called "Hidden". There may be some things about me that you know, but I don't. These things represent a "Blind" spot because I am unaware of them. Finally, there are some things about me that neither you nor I know. This area is called the "Unknown". I have added a qualification to the "Unknown" area by saying there are things unknown to us but known to God. It was probably the Unknown area that David was appealing to God to search out in him.

BLIND SPOTS

The Jo-Hari window is a helpful model in developing honesty and becoming more aware that some of our behaviors, attitudes, values, and motivations operate out of our awareness. When we have Blind spots, it is helpful to receive feedback from those around us whose opinion we trust and value. This is especially helpful when we are trying to discern whether we are hearing a word from God or the word is just the product of our own thinking. Peter was greatly used by God and could certainly hear God speak to him. Yet Paul had to point out some prejudices that were still present in Peter that had either gone ignored or were part of Peter's Blind area (Galatians 2:11-21).

HIDDEN AREAS

There is an old saying that goes something like this, "What you don't know can't hurt you." Hopefully, the fallacy in this statement is readily apparent. Our Hidden areas can leave us vulnerable to various character flaws such as shallowness, pretense, low self-esteem, inflated egos, and man pleasing dispositions. These become filters for the words we receive.

The story of Ananias and Sapphira taken from Acts 5:1-11 provides a dramatic example of two people who engaged in dishonesty due in part to their Hidden areas.

In the early church, many of the people who had become Christians lived together in community. They sold their possessions and shared all things in common with one another.

Ananias and his wife, Sapphira, sold their land and received payment for it. The difference with these two was that they did not want to give all the proceeds to the church. They were not being coerced in any way and to give or not to give was strictly their choice. However, they attempted to hide from the disciples their true feelings about giving the money. Together they conspired to lie and gave the disciples a false price for the sale of their property. They could then keep the rest of the money for themselves.

God revealed to Peter what they had done, and the results were tragic for them. Perhaps Ananias and Sapphira were well meaning people, but they concealed an important part of their awareness. The Bible does not give any insight as to what caused them to become so inauthentic and afraid of being who they really were. Perhaps they were distrusting of the spiritual leaders or afraid that their own needs would not be met. Maybe they didn't want to give up a certain life-style. We certainly have no answers for their behavior. However, it does seem as though there were some things in their heart that were out of their awareness. Their story lets us know that we must deal with our Hidden area and the secret agendas that control our behavior which can have the effect of contaminating how we hear and what we do.

THE UNKNOWN

The Unknown area represents things that are present but may not have surfaced to level of conscious awareness. It may take a unique situation such as a crisis for the unknown to become known to us. And sometimes when the Unknown becomes Known, it isn't what we expected to see. In a crisis, Job's wife encouraged him to curse God and die. Peter's response to his crisis was to lie three times. Abraham denied that Sarah was his wife.

Jeremiah 17:9 tells us, *"The heart is deceitful above all things and desperately wicked; Who can know it?"* Being able to see through our real heart motivations is challenging. Jeremiah suggests that this is something God must do for us. Jeremiah 17: 10 says, *"I, the Lord search the heart, even to give every man according to his ways, according to the fruit of his doings"*. Therefore, our protection from the Unknown is to seek God and come into agreement with David's prayer for Him to do what we cannot do, and that is to thoroughly search our hearts. And when He shows us what He sees, we are to ask Him to cleanse us from all unrighteousness. The pure in heart will be brought near to Him.

SUMMARY

The Jo-Hari model of awareness is a helpful tool to use in learning to identify the voice of self. It enables us to probe into the shadowed areas of our heart. Psalm 51:6 says, *"Behold You desire truth in the inward parts, and in the hidden part You will make me to know wisdom."* The idea here is that God delights and takes pleasure when His word reaches our hearts. He promises that even in the areas that are out of our consciousness He will increase wisdom. To hear the voice of God is to know the wisdom of God. When the searchlight of His word is shining upon and within us, we will be able to discern His voice clearly.

PRAYER

Dear God, make me more astute in recognizing the sound of my own voice. Reveal to me my Blind spots. I do not want to get blindsided as I pursue You. Make known the Hidden and Unknown areas so that I can continue to grow and mature in my daily walk with You. Amen.

PAUSE AND REFLECT

Based upon the teaching in this section, what is your understanding of the voice of the flesh?

How can we know when our good ideas are not God ideas?

Discuss the different parts of the Jo-Hari Window.

What parts of the Jo-Hari window do you feel are more applicable to you?

Discuss the saying, "What you don't know, won't hurt you".

What has God spoken to you through this chapter? Write it here.

Tell how you will apply the information in this section.

QUIET TIME: BE STILL AND KNOW

God speaks to an Unknown area of your life. What does He say and how do you feel about that? Write it here.

SPEAK LORD WORKSHEET

Refer to the last "Speak Lord Worksheet" that you completed. Has God spoken to you about the situation you described? If so, you may either skip this page or write about another concern.

1. One thing that I would like for God to speak to me about is:

2. This is what I feel that God has already spoken to me regarding my concern:

3. It is important for God to speak to me about this area of my life because:

4. This is what I will do in response to what God tells me:

CHAPTER 11

Discerning the Voice of the Flesh (Part 2)

"There is a way that seems right to a man,
but its end is the way of death." Proverbs 14:12

We serve a talking God. Essential to our quest to know the voice of God is to discern our thoughts from God's thoughts. This section will give more understanding in discerning the voice of the flesh.

REINING IN OUR THOUGHTS

If our thoughts naturally tend to be different from God's thoughts, how are we to get to the place wherein our thoughts and God's thoughts are on the same wavelength? Well, we must learn what things are okay to think about and meditate upon. Since God often speaks to us through our thought life, we need to keep this channel clear and open to Him. This means we are to guard our thought life. Philippians 4:8 provides useful insight as to how to accomplish this. Paul says *"Finally, my brethren whatever is true, whatever is noble, whatever is just, whatever is pure, whatever is lovely, whatever is of a good report, if there is any virtue and if there is anything praiseworthy-meditate on these things."*

WHATEVER IS TRUE

We are to live in reality. Truth portrays things as they really are. If we are in denial, we have a distorted perception of things. A distorted perception will affect how we hear. Jesus prayed for a blind man to receive his sight. After the first prayer, the man reported that he could see but his vision was not clear. His description of the people he saw was that they appeared to be *"trees walking."* Jesus prayed for him again and then the man reported he could see clearly (Mark 8:22-26). Our hearing can be distorted just like the blind man's perception if we do not develop a love for the truth.

When we meditate on the truth we will not live lives of falsehood. We will not be open to believe lies about fellow believers, about ourselves and about God. Eve meditated on the lie that the enemy told her about herself and God. She then brought Adam into bondage to the same lie.

Pilate in jest asked Jesus, *"What is truth?"* (John 18:38). Jesus had already answered this question in His prayer for the disciples where He said to the Father, *"Sanctify them by Your truth. Your word is truth"* (John 17:17). God's word is reality for the Christian. When we meditate on the truth of His word, we are saturating our mind with God's reality. Jesus said, *"Everyone who is of the truth hears My voice"* (John 18:37). A lover of truth will be able to hear God's voice.

WHATEVER IS NOBLE

Noble things are whatever we hold in high regard. They represent what we esteem highly. This term was originally used in reference to a god and so it also carries the idea of giving reverence. The princes of Israel were called nobles because of their status and position of high regard. In our thought life meditating on things that are noble means that we are reflecting upon things that have positive value to us.

What are your values? Your thought life will reveal your values. The choices you make will reveal your values. Jesus gave guidelines in the Beatitudes which reflect kingdom values. An example of this comes from Matthew 6:31-34. It reads, *"Therefore do not worry, saying, 'What shall we eat?' or 'What shall we drink?' or 'What shall we wear?' For after all these things the Gentiles seek. For your heavenly Father knows that you need all these things. But seek first the kingdom of God and His righteousness, and all these things shall be added to you. Therefore, do not worry about tomorrow, for tomorrow will worry about its own things. Sufficient for the day is its own trouble."*

Our thought life can be so consumed with cares about the natural man that we have little energy for meditating on the condition of the spiritual man. Paul said, *"If you then were raised with Christ, seek those things which are above, where Christ is, sitting on the right hand of God. Set your mind on things above, not on things on this earth"* (Col. 3:1-2). When our mind is set on things above, it means we have redirected our thoughts. We have ceased focusing on the things which are temporal and have redirected our thoughts to the things which are eternal.

WHATEVER IS JUST

We are to be fair and honest in our dealings with one another. Our thoughts ought to show our intent to serve each other and be a blessing. Unjust thoughts are avenues that lead to attempts at manipulation and control. As we meditate on whatever is just, we learn how to make judgments about our unjust deeds and thoughts when they show up in us. Micah 6:8 poses this question, *"...and what does the Lord require of you but to do justly, and to love mercy, and to walk humbly with your God?"*

WHATEVER IS PURE

How well we know the extent to which our minds can become dumping grounds for the garbage of thought impurity! Murders are conceived in the mind, sexual sins take root in the thought life, and unforgiveness and hatred are strongholds on our thought processes. These things represent only a few of the challenges we encounter to having pure thoughts. We are bombarded with impure stimuli throughout the day. Movies, television, cell phones, iPads and the internet invite us to engage in the forbidden things. Television and movies glamorize sin so that it is easy to buy into a distorted and deceptive view of morality. Our thoughts are experienced as safe places where we can fantasize about immoral practices. God wants to be God even in this area of our lives.

Pure implies the absence of mixture. A pure thing is 100% of whatever it claims to be. In our thought life, we are not to indulge in worldly contemplation at one time and spiritual thoughts at another time. When the children of Israel left Egypt, a group referred to as the mixed multitude went out with them (Exodus 12:38). The mixed multitude proved to be a stumbling block for the Israelites. They began to lust after some of the things they had in Egypt. As a result, the Israelites started complaining to God and Moses and begging for those same things (Numbers 11:4). The mixture in our thoughts will open us up to yearning for the old life. The Israelites soon forgot about the hard bondage of slavery in Egypt. It was then easy for Egypt to become glorified in their mind as the land of plenty.

Let us strive to have thoughts that are free of mixture. Through the power of Holy Spirit our thoughts can be pure as we wash our minds with Scripture. God's word will be the soap and water that we need to cleanse us from the temptation to engage in the secret sin.

WHATEVER IS LOVELY

Usually when we think of something being lovely it is linked to the idea of beauty, usually external beauty. This is not the meaning of the term as Paul uses it here. It means amicable or pleasing or lovable.

We are to meditate on things that are worthy of love. What things are worthy of our deepest affection? What thoughts transform us into lovely people? When we are difficult to live with or unpleasant to be around, it could be because of what we've meditated on. Pleasing thoughts about others and even ourselves, bring about a pleasant disposition. As Christians, we want to love what God loves. Those things are worthy of our deepest affection. God loves truth, justice, righteousness, purity, honesty, a willing heart and so many other things. As you study the Scriptures, make a note when you come across something that God loves. Then meditate on those things.

WHATEVER IS OF A GOOD REPORT

This refers to things within society or the world at large for which there exists a consensus regarding their value. It would include virtues such as kindness, respect for parents, generosity toward the poor and courtesy. It could also be reflected in our holding a high regard for institutions that endorse these virtues. We are to embrace values and norms in our culture, which are consistent with Biblical principles and to reject those which are not.

THINK ON THESE THINGS

Paul concludes the passage in Philippians 4:8 by saying, *"If there is any virtue, and if there is anything praiseworthy-meditate on these things."* Hopefully, it is recognized that Paul is not only emphasizing thoughts as related to the mind, but also the thoughts of our heart. The Scripture links the thought life and the heart together. Consider Proverbs 23:7 which reads, *"For as he thinks in his heart, so is he."*

If we review the list of things that Paul encourages us to meditate upon, it should be evident that these things reflect the character of Jesus. He is true, just, pure etc. He is to be the center of our thought life. When we train our minds to meditate on the things listed above, it makes hearing from God a natural part of our everyday life. It will give us more confidence in what we hear because we have eliminated some of the clogs in the channel of our mind. The thoughts of our heart with its imaginations, plans and devices are submitted to the witness of Holy Spirit. Holy Spirit can then flow freely through our thoughts impressing God's word into our hearts.

JESUS CHRIST, THE WISDOM OF GOD

In 1 Corinthians 1:30, we read, *"But of Him you are in Christ Jesus, who became for us wisdom from God, and righteousness, and sanctification and redemption."* Let us remember that God is the source of all wisdom and knowledge. We want Him to invade our thought life, so we can have God thoughts.

According to Philippians 2:5, we are to *"Let this mind be in you which was also in Christ Jesus."* We are not to let our thought life have reign over us, but practice bringing it into subjection to God's word. The mind of Christ is a mind of humility. We do not want to have ego-inflated thoughts about ourselves and what we can do. We must be quick to acknowledge our dependency on the wisdom of God to guide our lives.

SUMMARY

The voice of the flesh is when we attribute our own thoughts to the voice of God. A clear channel for God's voice to flow through is developed by directing our thought life toward the virtues discussed by Paul in Philippians 4:8. The voice of the flesh is probably the most difficult to discern because we fail to know the thoughts of our heart.

PRAYER

Lord, help me to bring my thought life into subjection to Philippians 4:8. Amen

PAUSE AND REFLECT.

Discuss each of the virtues of Philippians 4:8.

Tell of successes and struggles that you've experienced in trying to bring your thought life in line with these virtues.

How can you use the word of God to rein in your thoughts?

Read Philippians 2:5-11. Contrast this with Eve's desire for self-exaltation. Discuss this also in reference to 2 Corinthians 10:15.

Tell how you plan to use the information learned in this section. Be specific.

What has God spoken to you through this chapter? Write it here

BE STILL AND KNOW

God's voice is the voice of truth. What truth does He speak to you about Himself? What truth does He want you to know about you? Write it here.

CHAPTER 12

Discerning the Voice of the Enemy

"Beloved, do not believe every spirit, but test the spirits,
whether they are of God..." 1 John 4:1

We serve a talking God who reveals Himself to us by teaching us how to recognize His voice. Satan, as the enemy of God, competes with Him for our attention. In I John 4:1 we are given this admonition; *"Beloved, do not believe every spirit, but test the spirits whether they be of God; for many false prophets have gone out into the world."* Since there is a false or counterfeit of the true, we must be able to discern truth from error. We need to know how to distinguish the deceptive voice of the enemy from God's voice.

THE VOICE OF THE ENEMY

In 2 Corinthians 2:11 Paul says, *"For we are not ignorant of his* (satan's) *devices"* (parenthesis mine). We are to be informed about the nature and stratagems of our enemy. Satan is subtle and attempts to sabotage the purposes of God by becoming the voice of the stranger that leads us astray.

WE ARE NOT IGNORANT

The enemy has certain characteristics that give us clues about the nature of his communication. According to John 8:44, he is a **liar**. Lying is his basic mode of communicating. We do not expect the truth to come from him because truth will not come from a liar. James poses the question as to whether the same fountain can bring forth bitter and sweet water (James 3:11). Obviously, the answer is, "No, it can't." Neither can truth come from satan. When he speaks, he will speak a lie. That is why it is so crucial that we know the truth of God's Word that will unmask his lies.

Satan is also a **deceiver** (Revelation 20:3,10). A deceiver is one who makes things appear to be something that they are not. It is satan's job to try to deceive us. His primary motive is to deceive us about the nature of God. He will say, "God doesn't love you" or "God is getting tired of you" or "God knows you don't really love Him like you should." Satan is the enemy of God and his goal is to move us away from God in whatever way he can.

John 10:10 says, *"The **thief** does not come except to steal, and to kill and to destroy."* This means that the enemy of our souls is always up to no good and that he is deadly serious in his intent. He comes to steal. A thief takes away something that belongs to another person without asking their permission. He or she is not going to knock on your door and say, "May I take your smart phone, your DVD player, your golf clubs and your grandmother's china?" Neither will the enemy pull up a moving van in front of your spiritual house with a big sign that reads Robbery Moving Company and then politely ask you for your faith, your trust in God, your devotion time etc. The enemy did not secure Adam's or Eve's consent to come in and rob them. He stole their innocence, robbed them of their trust and plundered their confidence before God. The result was that their damaged spiritual house was left in the shambles of fear, guilt and shame.

The enemy is a **killer**. He wants to get rid of some things. He wants to wipe us out for keeps. So, he will continuously attack us in an effort to destroy in us the same types of things he destroyed in Adam and Eve. He took away their eternal life. They were confined to bodies that would wear out, grow old and eventually cease to be. Thank God, we have eternal life restored in Jesus Christ!

Yet, the enemy seeks to kill our union with God because he despises our relationship with God. He hates it when we are devoted worshippers and lovers of God. He is filled with rage at the thought of us spending eternity worshipping and adoring this wonderful, majestic and loving God. We must remember that satan not only hates God, but his desire is to be worshipped as God.

Satan is a **destroyer** and his goal is to render us less effective. If he cannot steal something from us or wipe us out, he will concentrate on making us less than what God destined us to be. Adam and Eve were rendered less effective because they began to live in fear. They did not have the same freedom or close relationship with God as they had once enjoyed.

The nature of the enemy makes it extremely important for us to discern his tactics. The good news is that there are some general principles that we can apply that will help assist us in this endeavor.

HOW IS GOD PRESENTED?

If what we hear reflects negatively on the character of God, it will be the voice of Satan. This presumes we have a Biblical basis for our knowledge of God. It is obvious that if we don't know what God is like, then it will be more difficult for us to discern. Satan sought to discredit God in the eyes of Adam and Eve. He implied that God was not being honest and was holding out on them. He also caused them to believe that God didn't want the best for them. Often satan casts doubt about God's character with some variation of an "if, then why" statement. "If God" is followed by some known attribute of God such as loving, good, kind etc. and "then, why" comes next in which the "why" is a reference to some situation which seems to belie God's true character. For example, "If God cared about you, then why didn't He stop the divorce?" Or "If God is so generous, then why are you still struggling financially?" Unless it is settled in our heart that God's nature is unchanging, we may fail to recognize this as satan's voice and innocently see it as the thoughts of our own heart.

We are told numerous times throughout Scripture, *"The Lord is good"*. Psalm 73:1 says, *"**Truly** God is good"* (emphasis mine). Goodness is the basic character of God. Jesus said, *"There is none good, except one, that is God'* (Matthew 19:17). In discerning the voice of God, the voice of the enemy or the voice of the flesh, know that God will always speak that which is congruent with the essence of His nature.

DOES IT LEGITIMIZE THE ILLEGITIMATE?

Satan's voice will encourage us to give in to fleshly desires. Fleshly desires are not to be limited to the desire for physical pleasures, but must include our quest for fame, fortune and power. Fleshly desires are often a response to the "I want" in us that stands in opposition to the "God wants" in us. Jesus was tempted of the devil when He was in the wilderness with the "I want" desires (Yes, He, too, had to discern the voice of satan).

The temptation of Jesus is recorded in Matthew 4:1-11. Satan came to Jesus and spoke with him. The nature of his conversation seemed designed to trap Jesus into legitimizing the illegitimate needs of the flesh by acting independently of God.

Satan's first temptation was to challenge the famished Savior to turn stones in the desert to bread. This would have been one way in which Jesus could have satisfied His hunger. Satan was saying to Jesus, "It's okay for you to turn these stones into bread because you are hungry. Hey, Jesus, this is a legitimate need you have. I'm concerned about you because you have been without food for so long. I'm with you. I know you're hungry. It's okay. Just use the power."

Jesus' response to satan showed that He had correctly discerned the enemy's voice and his motive as well. Jesus told Satan that we do not live by only eating bread or natural food, but we are required to live by every word that comes from God's mouth. The enemy was trying to gain an entrance in which his words to Jesus were equal with God's words to Him. Again, the subtle way in which he sought to accomplish this was to seek to get Jesus to legitimize the illegitimate. In other words, he wanted to get Jesus to agree that he did not need to consult with God about how to get His needs met.

In the second temptation, satan appealed to the fleshly need to grandstand and draw attention to self in ways that bring glory to the flesh. We all have within us a desire for greatness. That is why people climb mountains, go over Niagara Falls in a barrel or appear on American Ninja Warrior or The Voice. As Christians, any desire for greatness has to be submitted to the will of God for us. Satan wanted Jesus to put the Father in the position of proving something to Him and the world. Jesus, knowing that God had given Him power, did not stoop to legitimize satan's request. To challenge God in this way would not be an act of faith. Instead it would reflect the highest form of arrogance.

The third temptation was to take Jesus upon a high mountain and show Him all the kingdoms of the world. Satan promised to give Jesus these kingdoms if He would just worship him. In this temptation, his real desire, to be worshipped, is fully revealed. Anything that we hear that pulls us away from our worship of God is the voice of the enemy. Any voice that bids us worship something other than God, whether that takes the form of another person, an idea, material things or even our ministries, is the voice of Satan.

In these challenges, Jesus responded back with Old Testament Scripture. He knew His Father's character and His Father's voice. He quoted the Scripture to satan. And since the word of God is truth and satan is a liar, he had to leave Jesus alone. Satan tries to use the same age-old tactics on us. He will cast doubt on God's word or misinterpret the word to us. Please note that in each temptation, he used Scripture to try to seduce Jesus into legitimizing the illegitimate. A thorough knowledge of the Bible will help us to launch a counter attack. It is helpful to know the context of the Scripture as well as Scripture content.

In the encounter with satan Jesus provided us with an example of self- denial and discernment of fleshly motives. These virtues are an essential part of a godly life style. Observing them will help to heighten our ability to discern and resist the voice of the enemy.

WHERE DOES IT TAKE YOU?

The voice of Satan moves us away from God. It interrupts our Christian walk and we will find ourselves going astray. When God speaks to us, even if it is a corrective word, we should experience the desire is to seek Him and know Him in a deeper way. Satan brings words of condemnation and whispers that God will never forgive us for some mistake we made.

Satan's voice creates distance between God and us. Because of satan's influence on Adam and Eve to sin, we were separated from God. Isaiah prophesied, *"All we like sheep have gone astray; we have turned, every one into his own way; and the Lord has laid on Him the iniquity of us all* (Isaiah 53:6). Going in our own way is the opposite of walking in God's way. Satan seeks to get us to pursue our own plans, interests and pleasures. He shows us the path that seems right to us, but the result is alienation from God.

I remember years ago a friend and I were having a conversation. We were both young Christians at the time. She was sharing about a temptation she had recently experienced. She said, "I felt terrible about it. And when I thought about it, a voice said, 'You know you shouldn't have said that.' And I said, 'Yes, that's right.' And then the voice said, 'It was terrible what you did.' Again, I agreed with the voice. Next the voice said, 'now you can't pray or even call upon God'." My friend said when she heard that she said, "Oh, no! That's not true! And now I know who you are. You are satan and you are trying to keep me away from God."

Satan's condemning voice carries a death sentence. It brings death to the life that God has placed within. We lose our joy, our peace, and our confidence. We can lose our sense of God-given purpose. We may find that our desire to continue to advance in spiritual things is gone.

Satan is a loser who camouflages himself as a winner. A loser is not concerned about creating winners. As a loser, satan's goal is to duplicate himself. He was cast out of heaven and out of the presence of God because of sin and rebellion. He lost the most desirable thing in the entire world and now he is trying to withhold it from unsuspecting Christians. But, we, who were at one time walking away from God, are now brought near to God because of the blood of Jesus (Ephesians 2: 13). By the blood of Jesus, we are reconciled to God and this same blood is our weapon against our adversary. The blood says we are now accepted by God because of the sacrifice of His Son.

Satan tries to trip us up in any way that he can. Holy Spirit is our helper in uncovering the snares he places in our path. We can discern his voice and turn aside as we respond to that other voice, which is the voice of God.

ARE YOU UNDER PRESSURE?

Satan's voice often brings a feeling of pressure to act. We turn to an incident in the life of David to bring clarity about this. In 1 Chronicles 21:1 we read, "*And Satan stood up against Israel and provoked David to number Israel.*" The first thing we want to observe is that satan's battle was with Israel, God's chosen people. If his battle is with God's people, then it is with God. The battles we encounter as satan tries to control the spiritual airwaves of our mind is because we, too, are God's chosen people. We are a part of something much larger than we can imagine. Any attack against you is an attack against the kingdom of God which is in you.

The next thing we want to observe is that satan provoked David. He stirred up something in David that caused him to make a decision independently of God. This was not typical behavior for the man who is described as after God's own heart (Acts 13:22). When there is pressure to move in a certain direction and you are not allowed time to reflect upon it, question the voice that is speaking. God is not a high pitch salesperson who is asking us to sign on the dotted line before we have any real understanding of what is transpiring.

IS IT CONSISTENT WITH GOD'S DEALING?

Over time we can gain an understanding of the pattern of God's dealings in our life. Eventually, it will become clear that God is consistent in the way that He deals with us. Occasionally He may lead us in a way that we have not gone before. However, even at those times, we can still find a degree of consistency if we look for the pattern. Therefore, when the voice we hear is leading us into something that seems foreign and unfamiliar, we would do well to question that voice.

There is a story in the Old Testament about a prophet that God sent on a mission. He was given clear instructions about what he was to do and exactly how to do it. One aspect of his instructions contained an unusual caution against having a meal during his trip. He obeyed God and went where he was told to go, delivered his message and started back home. So far, so good. However, before he reached home, he encountered another prophet who entreated him to have a meal with him. In disobedience to God's word he yielded to the pressure of the other prophet and ate the meal. Immediately afterwards God spoke judgment against him (1 Kings 13:1-31).

When God has spoken clearly, would He speak something in which He contradicts Himself? The answer is obvious. He wouldn't. There may be times when we are sure we have heard clearly from God and then start to think He is speaking something entirely different than what we heard initially. Remember the rule in college for the multiple choice and true and false tests? We were told to go with our first answer and not to go back and second-guess what we had chosen. Well, this works on the spiritual side also. Know how God deals with you and be alert to anything that seems contrary to the known dealings of God in your life.

PUTTING IT IN PERSPECTIVE

James gives us a passage of Scripture that will help us put things into perspective. James describes two types of wisdom. In this section, we will look at the first type. This is the voice of wisdom that does not come from God. James says, *"Who is wise and understanding among you? Let him show by good conduct that his works are done in meekness of wisdom. But if you have bitter envy and self-seeking in your hearts, do not boast and lie against the truth. This wisdom does not descend from above, but is earthly, sensual, demonic. For where envy and self-seeking exists there will be confusion and every evil thing will be there"* (James 3: 13-15).

James makes a connection between ungodly wisdom and the condition of the heart. The heart is linked to the ears in ways we do not fully understand. Perhaps similarly to the relation between the heart and the mouth. Jesus said the mouth was the voice for the heart (Matthew 12:34). Could it be that out of the heart, the ears hear? The sounds that our ears hear will have a clarity level and a purity level consistent with the purity level of our heart.

We are required to examine our hearts and check to see whether those things James cites are present. He specifically mentions envy and self-seeking as indicative of pride and falsehood. Remember, the voice of satan does not speak God's truth. The presence of bitterness, envy and strife leave us open to the voice of satan. These things do not reflect the character of Christ. However, they do reflect the very nature of satan. We must free ourselves from these so that we can hear a pure word. The voice of satan comes to feed these negative emotions and attitudes when they are in us. The voice of the enemy will direct our focus to the things of this world. It will speak to us concerning fleshly indulgences and it will be evil in its intent.

WHAT FRUIT?

Jesus said that a tree would be known by the fruit it produced (Matthew 12:33). He said a good tree will not bear bad fruit and a bad tree cannot produce good fruit. Knowing this provides a way for us to test the voice that has spoken to us to determine its source. We can do this by asking, "How is my life different because of having heard this voice? What fruit is produced in my life?"

If we are around people who build us up and encourage us in our walk with the Lord, we will most likely be stronger in our faith. On the other hand, if we are constantly being torn down and told what miserable Christians we are we may begin to doubt our salvation. One set of voices produces the good fruit of faith; the other set produces the bad fruit of doubt and unbelief.

The voice of satan produces negative fruit such as confusion. Confusion is when we are not clear in our thinking. It's as if our mind is in turmoil and we can't sort out our thoughts. The Bible says, "*For God is not the author of confusion, but of peace*" (I Corinthians 14:33).

The voice of satan also stirs up fear and anxiety. When Goliath challenged the armies of Israel they were terrified, weakened and immobilized by his threatening words (1 Samuel 17:4-10). On the other hand, when God speaks to us we will experience peace, have clear direction and feel stronger spiritually. We will feel built up rather than torn down and trampled upon.

One word used to express the idea of being built up is "edify" (see Romans14:29; 1 Corinthians 10:23; 1 Thessalonians 5:11). Edify is related to edifice which is our word for building. The children of Israel were torn down by Goliath's words. It was like a wrecking crew had come in and demolished a building. We are God's building, a holy habitation in which He dwells. He will always speak words that build us up.

Another fruit produced by satan is pride. The voice of satan praises the fleshly man and thus inflates our ego. We are told Holy Spirit does not even speak of Himself, but all that He says glorifies Jesus (John 16:13). The voice of satan does not speak anything that exalts Jesus as Lord.

The voice of satan will not produce the fruit of steadfastness. When we listen to his voice, we tend to be shaky in our experience, wavering and unable to make decisions. This is what it means to be double minded. Double-minded persons will be unstable in all their ways (James 1:8). They will not be able to stay on the right course but will be like ships that are tossed about in the sea by the wind. We are exhorted to be *"steadfast, immoveable, always abounding in the work of the Lord"* (1 Corinthians 15:58).

SUMMARY

The voice of the enemy comes to turn us aside from the path of righteousness. We can learn to discern his voice so that we will not confuse it with the voice of God. It is important to know the character of God because His dealings with us are always consistent with His character. Several questions were posed that can be used as an essential tool in discerning the enemy's voice. We can expect to know the source of the communication by the fruit it produces in our life.

PRAYER

Father, I thank You that I can know when you speak to me. Amen.

PAUSE AND REFLECT

Are there ways in which satan has attempted to steal, kill, or destroy something God has given you?

How does the voice of Satan lead you away from God?

Discuss each of the topical questions asked in this chapter.

Review James 3:13-15. Discuss it in more detail.

Tell how you will apply the information learned in this chapter.

What has God spoken to you through this chapter? Write it here.

BE STILL AND KNOW

Jesus came that you might experience overflowing life. God speaks life into a certain area of your heart. What is He saying? Write it here.

CHAPTER 13

Discerning the Voice of God

"And when he brings out his own sheep, he goes before them, and the sheep follow him, for they know his voice. Yet they will by no means follow a stranger, for they do not know the voice of strangers."
John 10: 4, 5

We serve a talking God who has spoken to us through His written word, the Bible. What He has spoken will forever stand because as an eternal God His word is also eternal. Thus, the written word of God becomes the reference point for all personal communication received from Him. We are to apply the word test to all communication we feel may be from God.

THE WORD TEST

We have identified the Bible as our textbook for gaining knowledge about hearing the voice of God. The Bible tells us what God has already said. This is the information that He has deemed essential for us to know regarding His purpose for the universe and all its inhabitants. In it we find words of ageless wisdom addressing the basic things that concern us all. The various attributes with which we define ourselves and use as the basis of our identity do not prevent the Bible from having relevance for all people. The Bible transcends cultures, ethnicity, race, age, and gender.

Students are taught to review the textbook in preparation for an exam. This is because a thorough knowledge of the text is highly critical to passing the exam. We, too, must know what the Bible says so that we may be better prepared to deal with the tests and trials that come our way.

When satan approached Jesus in the wilderness (refer again to Matthew 4:1-11), he tempted Him in several different ways. To each temptation, Jesus replied, "*It is written*" followed by quotations from the books of the Law. Jesus had to know what God had said to discern that the voice He heard was not speaking God's will for Him.

During the temptation, Jesus was in three diverse environments. However, that did not change the way He responded. He continued to apply the word test. We often find ourselves in different and unique circumstances and situations. The Israelites had trouble believing God could meet their needs in various conditions. He supplied water for them in the wilderness, but at another time when they had no meat, they questioned His ability to provide for them again. We must remember that we can hear the voice of God in any place and at any time. The word of the Lord will come back to us as an anchoring point for our current situation or circumstance.

Satan tempted Jesus at three different times. Often the enemy just does not give up. He keeps pressing against us in the attempt to wear us out and to cause us to give in. One thing we can learn from the temptation of Jesus is that no matter how often the enemy approaches us, the word of God does not decrease in strength and power. Jesus continued to respond with "*It is written*". God's voice is constant and consistent.

Remember the Old Testament prophet in 1 Kings 13:11-18 that was discussed in the previous chapter? He did not fully apply the word test to the message he received from the false prophet. Because the person telling him to do something different said he was a prophet also, he placed more importance on that person's position and title than he did on what God had told him. Therefore, Paul warns us, "*But even if we, or an angel from heaven, preach any other gospel to you than we have preached to you, let him be accursed"* (Galatians 1:8). The word of God can be used consistently and confidently over multiple trials and temptations.

Jesus was tempted in three areas of needs. The enemy tempted Him to change what God had said to get His needs meet in a fleshly way. Even though the Lord had spoken to Abraham and Sarah and promised to make them a great nation, they were childless for many years. When the manifestation of the promise was delayed, Sarah took matters into her own hands. She got her need to have a child met through resorting to a fleshly solution (see Genesis 16).

Her desire to give birth was a God-given longing, but Sarah did not apply the word test. The promise of God was that *she* would give birth to their heir and not Hagar. Giving Hagar, her servant, to Abraham so that she could have a child seemed to Sarah like the right thing to do. Unfortunately, it resulted in unforeseen consequences for their descendants then and now.

We are to always apply the word test because we don't always know if the choices we are faced with are right or wrong. The word of God will bring clarity in this area. Even when something sounds right, the word of God will enable us to discern the truth.

THE WORD WILL TEST

Hebrews 4:12 reads, *"For the word of God is living and powerful and sharper than any two-edged sword, piercing even to the division of soul and spirit, and joint and marrow, and is a discerner of the thoughts and intents of the heart."*

Please note that the word of God is described as "living and powerful". It is active in its effort to accomplish what God intends. In Isaiah 55:11, God speaks through the prophet saying, *"So shall my word be that goes forth from my mouth; it shall not return to me void, but it shall accomplish what I please, and it shall prosper in the thing for which I sent it.*" We may engage in idle chatter, but this is not the nature of God. When He speaks, it is with thoughtful intent.

God's words will bring life to the hearer. Even when God speaks a corrective word, He appends it with a word of redemption whereby we may continue to hope and not loose heart. The word of God is not oppressive as in taking life from us. It will build us up so that we can continue to grow and prosper in Him. God's word is mighty and full of power. The words He speaks are lively and carry creative energy which causes them to bring about the manifestation of whatever He speaks.

God's word is compared to a two-edged sword. The more literal translation is two-mouthed sword. Two-mouthed sword refers to the image of a sword as devouring everything before it. The Roman sword had two edges making it easier to cut in every direction. The word of God penetrates our heart in a similar fashion. It goes deep and exposes our motives and desires whether they are good or evil. God's word addresses and deals with the deepest and most secret areas of our heart.

God's word not only penetrates, it also divides. The deeper the word penetrates the more it divides. Therefore, it appears that without this deep penetration of God's word into our heart the work of the word in us is hindered. God's word divides the soul and the spirit. It will uncover within us our base desires and separate us unto the highest purpose that He holds for us. The priests of the Old Testament would take a knife and skillfully cut through a sacrificial animal carefully severing the various parts of the carcass. Paul's description of God's word is used to convey to us that the word of God is designed to have the same effect in our lives. It comes to divide the pure from the impure. Jesus declared, *"Do not think that I came to bring peace on earth. I did not come to bring peace but a sword"* (Matthew. 10:34). That sword was none other than His word that possessed the power to lay all things naked and bare.

The word of God is a discerner of the thoughts and intents of our heart. As said before, to discern means to discriminate and make a judgment about something. There is nothing so perfect for discerning our heart as the word of God. When we apply it to all aspects of our lives, we are then empowered to discern. What is better than the word of God to give us spiritual discernment to know His voice and distinguish it from the voice of self and the voice of the enemy?

TESTED BY THESE QUESTIONS

Is what you hear consistent with what is in the written word, the Bible? We have already noted that God will speak in conjunction with what He has already said. God does not use the same means of verifying His word, as we would use. We would call in multiple witnesses. He bears witness to Himself. He testifies to what He Has said.

Does it glorify Jesus Christ? In all that is said and done, Jesus is to be exalted. He is the One who is worthy of the glory, honor and praise. When there is a focus on the person and how God is using that person, this is most likely the voice of the flesh. Of course, God will encourage us from time to time by reminding us of the gifts He has given to us and the unique work that He has for us to do. However, when we exalt the gifts and the call above the Gift Giver and the Caller, we are yielding to the voice of self.

Is what you hear in line with the nature of God? God's word or voice to us will underscore His character. It will produce the fruit of the Spirit.

Does it bring you closer to God? There are times when God's words will convict us and we may experience godly sorrow. That godly sorrow will not lead us away from Him. Paul said, "*For godly sorrow produces repentance, leading to salvation, not to be regretted; but the sorrow of the world produces death*" (2 Corinthians 7:10).

Does what you hear make sense? Yes, there are times when God has told someone to do something strange, but this is the exception rather than the rule. For all intents and purposes, God is very practical. He has established an order in the universe and does not tend to violate His own sense of order.

Is what you hear consistent with God's dealings in your life? This simply points to the constancy and the consistency of God's word. God does not run around saying "no" at one time and then three minutes or three weeks later saying, "I didn't mean that. I really meant yes." That would really be confusing! And we know that God is not the initiator of confusion in our life. Therefore, we are to look for an ongoing pattern in the dealings of God with us.

TESTED BY THE FRUIT

James 3:17 reads, *"But the wisdom that is from above is first pure, then peaceable, gentle, willing to yield and full of mercy and good fruits, without partiality and without hypocrisy."*

God's words are first described as being pure. They will have a purifying effect on our lives cleansing us from sin and whatever else is in us that is displeasing to Him. Pure relates to the effect of God's words upon our mind. They can make our thoughts pure. Pure also means to be free from blame. His words will free us from guilt and condemnation through cleansing our conscience. Jesus said, *"You are already clean because of the word that I have spoken to you"* (John 15:3).

The word God speaks will release the fruit of peace. The enemy cannot counterfeit the peace of God. When the disciples were concerned about the future, Jesus promised to give them a peace that the world could not give. He reminded them not to be anxious about things. Psalm 119:165 says, *"Great peace have those who love your law, and nothing causes them to stumble."* As we cherish the words which God speaks to us, we will begin to trust Him more and more. His word will flood us with light and we will be able to walk in a peaceful way. His words are like gentle breezes that calm us and bring us to a place of rest.

God's word is gentle. It has been aptly said that God is a gentleman. He is not offensive. He does not say things to embarrass us or to cause us to experience shame. Another aspect of God's gentleness is that He doesn't coerce or force us into an action or response. He has given us a will whereby we can choose our responses. He will always be respectful of this. Remember, God will not act in violation of something established by Him. God is love and His nature is to love us into obedience.

The word of God is easily entreated. This wisdom causes us to be willing to yield to good counsel. We are not filled with doubt and unbelief which could lead to stubbornness and rebellion. This means that God's word is easy to receive. When we hear God speak, we should not experience a great internal struggle trying to decide whether or not God is speaking. We don't have to try to make some word we heard fit a situation when it obviously does not. That would be like buying a pair of shoes that were too little or too big. God knows our size. He knows the word to speak regarding our situation. When that word is spoken to our heart we will know it.

God's communication with us will reveal His mercy and produce the fruit of the Spirit in our life. Mercy is one of the enduring characteristics of God and His mercy pursues us all the days of our life. In 2 Corinthians 1:3, God is called the *"Father of all mercies."* He is the source or fountain from which mercy springs. This mercy will be evident when God speaks to us. God's word will be instrumental in developing in us the desire for righteous living. Our lives should be different in a positive way from having communicated with Him. When we hear the voice of God, our life will bear witness to it. If we are joyless, thankless, irritable, and full of unbelief and doubt, perhaps we are not listening to God's voice. We refer again to the creative aspect of God's word that brings life. It is through the word that we are conformed to His likeness.

His word is without partiality. It is not ambiguous so that we are constantly questioning its source or seeking to understand it. Neither is it applied unequally. The Bible contains words that speak to all.

God's wisdom is without hypocrisy. Hypocrisy relates to pretense and shame. God's word stands in stark contrast to this because it is truth. God will speak messages of truth to our heart. Hypocrisy is deceit and will hide the true character of a person. God's word as truth unveils and reveals our true character and works righteousness within.

SUMMARY

The Bible is our test manual for learning to recognize God's voice. The greater the knowledge we have of the Bible intellectually and experientially, the more skillful we will be in knowing God's voice. This is because God will always speak according to the written word. The Bible is our safety net that prevents us from falling into deception and error.

Seven attributes describe the wisdom from above. It is *pure, then peaceable, gentle, willing to yield and full of mercy and good fruits, without partiality and without hypocrisy."* Seven, symbolically, is God's perfect number. Perfect wisdom comes from above and God will give it to us if we ask Him. The only requirement is that we ask in faith. *"But let him ask in faith, with not doubting, for he who doubts is like a wave of the sea driven and tossed by the wind" (James 1:6).*

PRAYER

Today, I ask for the wisdom which comes from above. Amen.

PAUSE AND REFLECT

Describe how the "word test" can be applied across different environments, time and needs.

How does the word of God test the Christian?

What are some of the questions that you can ask to help determine if God is speaking to you?

In what areas are you experiencing the fruit of wisdom growing in your life?

What has God spoken to you through this chapter? Write it here.

How will you use the information shared in this chapter?

BE STILL AND KNOW

God will speak a Scripture to you heart. What do you hear? Write it here.

CHAPTER 14

Positioned to Hear

"But who has stood in the council of the Lord, and has perceived and heard His word? Who has marked His word and heard it?"
Jeremiah 23:18

We serve a talking God who has made it possible for us to communicate with Him. The very thought of this should fill us with incredible joy. The idea that God desires to talk to us is great news, isn't it? Then, why aren't we making ourselves available to have conversations with Him?

WHO

Jeremiah asked a penetrating question, *"But who has stood in the council of the Lord, and has perceived and heard His word? Who has marked His word and heard it?"* (Jeremiah 23:18). The context of Jeremiah's question was a discourse in which he pointed out some of the differences between true and false prophets. At that time, there were people claiming to be prophets and speaking for God but who were, in fact, just speaking out of their own heart. Jeremiah attempted to prove that they could not have heard the voice of God because they had not been in God's presence. He does not state this directly, but introduces the idea by asking "Who?" The image also comes to mind of an instructor looking eagerly for a student to raise a hand in response to a question that has been posed.

Who is that person? When the woman with the issue of blood touched Jesus, He asked, *"Who touched Me?"* (Luke 8:45). The disciples were somewhat perplexed by His question. After all, there was a crowd of people who were pushing up against them. Anyone in the crowd who got close to them could have touched Him. Jesus then made it clear that it was not simply a touch from contact with the passing crowd, but someone had touched Him intentionally. *"Who touched Me?"* then must be a search for identity.

God through Jeremiah conducts a similar identity search. We must take note that Jeremiah does not give possible suggestions as to the identity of the person. He does not say, "Who among you fathers?" or "Who among you leaders in Israel?" or "Who among the Levites?" He simply asks "Who?" That leaves us to identify the person or the person to identify himself/herself.

We could ask what man, woman, boy, girl, preacher, missionary, teacher, homemaker, etc. Am I the answer to "Who?" Are you? Since Jeremiah does not tell us who the person is, then it could be anybody. That seems to be the point that he wants to make. What will follow in his message could apply to any one of us.

WHO HAS STOOD?

Jeremiah gives us more information to put into our search engine as we look for the identity of the unknown person. The person he seeks is someone who has stood in the presence of the Lord. The word "stood" as used in this context relates to continuing and abiding. A reference to Jonah 1:3 will serve to amplify the meaning. We are told that Jonah rose up to flee to Tarshish *"from the presence of the Lord."* This means he fled from standing before God as His servant and minister. He was no longer submitted to God in obedience and removed himself from being in the place where God could speak to him.

In 1 Samuel 1:8-18, the story is told of Hannah, mother of the prophet Samuel. Hannah was barren, and the cry of her heart was to have a child. On one occasion, she left the religious festivities, her family and friends to go to the temple to seek God. Hannah went into the temple because she had a desperate need to hear what God had to say about her situation. As she in desperation sought God, she became an example of someone standing in the presence of the Lord. Now, her actual physical posture may have been in a kneeling or prone position. Standing in the presence of God from Jeremiah's perspective is not limited to physical stance. It is a committed attitude toward remaining in God's presence with a determination to hear Him speak to you.

Standing in the presence of God also relates to a ministerial position. Elijah and Elisha would introduce themselves with some version of this statement; *"As the Lord of hosts lives before whom I stand"* (see 1 Kings 17:1; 1 Kings 18:15 and 2 Kings 3:14). They were identifying their ministry as a prophet and with that the recognition that their ministry required them to continually position themselves before God.

WHO HAS STOOD IN THE COUNCIL?

A council refers to a place of secret confidential communication that has developed out of an intimate relationship with a person. This is the type of relationship that Peter, James and John enjoyed with Jesus. He would pull them aside and share things with them that he did not share with the other disciples. It also seems to be the type of relationship that Queen Esther had with her seven maidens. When she was at a time of crisis she called them together and shared the deepest concerns of her heart.

Deuteronomy 29:29 says. *"The secret things belong to the Lord our God, but those things which are revealed belong to us and to our children forever, that we may do all the words of this law,"* God will communicate even the secret things. He said, *"Shall I hide from Abraham what I am doing?"* (Genesis 18:17). God did not keep from Abraham His plans regarding the destruction of Sodom and Gomorrah. As a result, Abraham warned his nephew Lot, who could escape.

Abraham was called the friend of God. We should all seek a level of intimacy with God wherein He is delighted to call us friends. Jesus told His followers, "*I call you friends because all the things that I heard from my Father I have made known to you*" (John 15:15). As we come into a more intimate relationship with Him we are invited into that council of friends. Out of intimacy with Him we will hear more clearly.

WHO HAS PERCEIVED HIS WORD?

Perception means to understand what is being spoken. Perception is connected to revelation and being given the ability to see or to cause to see. In Isaiah 6:10, we read, "*Make the heart of this people dull, and their ears heavy, and shut their eyes; lest they see with their eyes, and hear with their ears, and understand with their heart, and return and be healed.*" According to this Scripture, to see with the eyes means a person hears and comprehends God's word and as a result of this will turn to Him. By way of contrast when a person's heart is hardened, it is as if they have shut their eyes and stopped up their ears and turned away from God.

Jeremiah's question is further directed to the person who wants to see (understand) and experience the word of God at work in their lives as a catalyst for change. That person believes the word to the point of accepting it. It is more than just hearing the word as James describes in James 1: 23, 24. James says, "*For if anyone is a hearer of the word and not a doer, he is like a man observing his natural face in a mirror; for he observes himself, goes away and forgets what kind of man he was.*" Hearing the word and not behaviorally responding to it means one is not allowing the word to do its intended purpose. James adds, "*But he who looks into the perfect law of liberty and continues in it, and is not a forgetful hearer but a doer of the word, this one shall be blessed in what he does.*"

WHO HAS MARKED HIS WORD?

Paying close attention to what is being spoken conveys the idea of "marking" the word of God. It denotes the active process of hearing. The more distractions in our life, the more difficult it will be for us to hear. We are to minimize the noisiness of our lives so that we can easily tune into the voice of God. Our prayer is that God will daily show us how to do this. Again, the emphasis is on hearing followed by obedience to whatever God speaks. Jeremiah's question is actually an answer. It is the answer to the question, "How do I hear from God?"

IT'S ME O' LORD

We should strive to be the answer to the prophet's question. We want to be found in the presence of the Lord being attentive to hear His every word. God is raising up a group of people who greatly desire to know Him in a deeper, more intimate way. These are the ones who stay in His presence and hear the secret of His heart revealed to them. They cherish the words that fall from His lips knowing they provide guidance and direction for their lives. Are you part of this hungry for God generation?

SUMMARY

Coming into God's presence during our devotional times puts us in position for God to speak to us. The act of hearing God's voice carries with it an expectation that the hearer will walk in obedience to whatever God says. Any child of God can hear the voice of God.

PRAYER

Lord, I want to be the answer to Jeremiah's question, "Who?" Teach me what it means to stand in Your counsel and to hear Your word. Let me be positioned to hear. Thank You that I can hear Your voice. Amen.

PAUSE AND REFLECT

What does it mean to be positioned to hear?

Tell how the concept of the hearing position relates to this chapter.

How will you position yourself to hear from God?

"Standing", "perceiving", "hearing", and "marking" are different steps to learning to hear the voice of God on a regular basis. Define each of these terms and then identify where you are in the process.

What has God spoken to you through this chapter? Write it here.

Tell how you will use the information in this section.

BE STILL AND KNOW

You have met the talking God. What do you want to say to Him? Write it here.

What is His response to you? Write it here.

SPEAK LORD WORKSHEET

Refer to the last "Speak Lord Worksheet" that you completed. Has God spoken to you about the situation you described? If so, you may either skip this page or write about another concern.

1. One thing that I would like for God to speak to me about is:

2. This is what I feel that God has already spoken to me regarding my concern:

3. It is important for God to speak to me about this area of my life because:

4. This is what I will do in response to what God tells me:

APPENDIX 1

Speak Lord Worksheet Explanation

1. One thing that I would like for God to speak to me about is:

    This statement is designed to help you to set a goal. Use it as a practice exercise for testing the hearing skills you will learn as you study this book. You may choose to ask God to speak to you about a current area of concern or something that is more long standing. An example of current issues would be dealing with a disgruntled employee, medical decisions, where to go on vacation, changing churches, or what college to attend. A long-standing question may relate to your ministry, marriage, career choices, a family situation. Either way, try to settle on a single issue.

    You will be given opportunities to refer to your goal periodically throughout the book. Continue to remain focused on the concern you initially identified until you feel God has spoken to you about it. Do not become anxious. Rest in the knowledge that God will speak to you because He is interested in every part of your life.

2. This is what I feel that God has already spoken to me regarding my concern:

    Has God already spoken something to you about your situation or are you completely in the dark? If God has spoken, indicate what you feel He said to you. Be sure to tell how you heard the voice of God and when.

If God has not spoken anything about it, indicate that as well. In this section, please share how frequently you have inquired of the Lord regarding your situation.

3. It is important for God to speak to me about this area of my life because:

This statement helps you to establish the degree of importance you have given your situation. This statement will also guide you toward anticipating the result of having heard the voice of God. When God speaks to you, what will be different? How will the situation or your life change?

4. What will you do in response to what God has said?

When God speaks, you are to respond in some way. This indicates that you are aware that He has spoken to you. A response can be verbal or behavioral or both. The response you make is determined by what was communicated to you.

APPENDIX 2

Hearing from God
Worksheet Explanation

1. *God has a language.* Throughout the Bible we encounter the various ways in which God has used to communicate with His people. Dreams, visions, an audible voice, a still small voice, prophets, teachers, angels, mind pictures, pastors and, of course, the written Word are only a few examples of how we experience the language of God.

Over time it should be evident that there is a consistent way in which the voice of God comes to you. For example, do you dream a lot? Do you love to spend time in reading the Bible and often have a Bible verse come to you to provide instruction, comfort or direction? Do you see visions? If either of these examples describes the way God speaks to you most of the time, then it would be an example of your *primary language.*

God can speak to you in more than one way. Maybe your *primary language* is dreams, but God also speaks to you through a still small voice or through impressing something upon your heart. Whatever is the second most consistent way God speaks to you, is your *secondary language.* Remember the *secondary language* can be just as strong as the *primary language.* It is labeled secondary only because it occurs less often than the primary. There are some persons who seem to have *two primary languages.*

2. Your *spiritual theme* relates to the dealings of God in your life over time. It may reflect some aspects of the character of our Lord. It could also be related to some area in your life in which He wants you to mature. You can identify your *spiritual theme* by asking these questions: What message seems to have been echoed to you throughout your Christian life? What message speaks to you no matter how often you hear it? What are the messages in a song or a sermon or in the Word that continually ministers to you? Some *spiritual themes* are giving, helping others, death to flesh, worship, spiritual warfare, the love of God, obedience, spiritual intimacy etc.

3. The concept of the *hearing position* relates back to the teaching on Samuel. It is the spiritual, physical, and emotional frequency at which your hearing is the clearest. Your *spiritual hearing pos*ition could be when you're in worship or prayer or just waiting in the presence of the Lord like Samuel in the temple. The *physical hearing position* relates to where you are at the time God speaks. Samuel was lying down on a cot or bed. Some people say God speaks to them when they are in the shower or driving their car or sitting in their favorite chair. Your *emotional state* also affects the clarity of your hearing. Some people can hear from God when they are in desperate straits as the woman with the issue of blood and Samuel's mother, Hannah. Others are in a more relaxed frame of mind which seems to have been the case with Samuel.

4. Samuel heard God speak to him somewhere between midnight and 4:00 a.m. It is not unusual for someone to say, "The Lord wakes me up every morning at 1:00 a.m." This is probably their *hearing time frame.* Your *hearing time frame* is the period during the day when you can hear more clearly. It could be morning, noon, night or some other time. Some *hearing time frames* are very specific, as in a certain hour. Others may be a range of time, as from 1:00 AM-3AM.

5. In learning to hear the voice of God, it is not unusual to run into *static*. *Static* is defined as anything that interferes with our ability to hear. Examples of *static* would be extreme busyness, fatigue, doubt, frustration, prayerlessness, not studying the Bible, etc. The goal is to identify the source of *static* and then rid yourself from as much of it as you can.

6. *Confirmation* can come in several different ways. Have you ever read something in the Bible only to go to church the next Sunday and hear the pastor quote the exact same Scripture as the text for the sermon? Well, that was *confirmation!* Another example would be when you feel God has spoken something to your heart and you get a phone call from a friend who shares the same thing with you. The experience of having the word God spoke to you come to pass is still another way in which *confirmation* occur.

Generally, we will probably most often experience confirmation as a sense of peace and quiet assurance in our heart. Psalm 85:8 says, *"I will hear what God the LORD will speak, for He will speak peace to His saints..."* This peace will be evident as we go about the daily routine of life seeking to live in conformity to the will of God. Isaiah said, *"The work of righteousness will be peace, and the effect of righteousness, quietness and assurance forever."* (Isaiah 32:17).

APPENDIX 3

Dealing with Distractions During Quiet Time or Prayer

In this section, I will discuss some ways that can help you to stay more focused and motivated during your quiet times with the Lord.

1. Worship music. Start your quiet time with music. I have found that this gives me a point of focus as I listen to the songs.

2. Racing thoughts. One of the primary ways distraction comes during our quiet times is with racing thoughts. Amazing, isn't it how we suddenly remember everything on our perpetual "to do" list. What I have learned to do is to keep pen and paper nearby. If I think of something that needs attending to, I just jot it down and then go back into prayer.

3. Phone calls. Decide whether you will take a phone call. Once you have made this decision, you will not need to worry each time the phone rings. You may want to let all calls go to voice mail. If you are concerned about emergencies, put the phone on "speaker" and that way you can screen your calls.

4. Praying the word. Choosing a Scripture as a point of prayer is very useful too. It provides an opportunity for you to pray that Scripture over your circumstances.

5. Few admit it, but one of the biggest distractions people experience during their quiet time is boredom. Examine your expectations for prayer. It is helpful to see it as a time to be in God's presence even though there are no earthquakes are glory clouds all around. Ask the Lord to help you to know the beauty of a quiet spirit in His presence.

If you still find yourself struggling with boredom, try keeping a prayer journal. Start praying about specific things and keep note of the progress that you see. As you experience God as a prayer answering God, you will become more motivated in your prayer time.

Remember, your quiet time is not measured by how much time you spend, but how you spend your time. Boredom during quiet time is often caused by the feeling that you need to devote an unreasonable amount of time to it. When you are not able to stay focused, for the time you set, it can lead to frustration as well as boredom. Start out with a time that seems manageable, even if it's just five minutes a day. You can always increase it.

APPENDIX 4

Bible Study FAQs

Why study the Bible?

It is important to make Bible Study a part of your daily spiritual discipline. A sound knowledge of God's Word is basic for learning to hear His voice. His Word is the foundation and so becomes your starting point. As you journey toward becoming more proficient in hearing God's voice, you will recognize His voice as the written Word begins to invade your thought life. A Bible verse that you read during your time of study will come back to you. When you meditate, or reflect upon that verse, God will give you wisdom and help you to apply it to your life.

What version of the Bible should I use?

At one time the most readily available version of the Bible was the King James Version. Now there are many different translations of the Bible from which to choose. It is probably a good idea to have more than just one. You could go to a Bible book store and spend some time browsing through different translations. Choose a Scripture and then compare it across translations. You could also use a parallel Bible which gives about 3 or 4 translations in the same Bible.

Where should I begin?

People sometimes ask where the best place is to begin Bible Study. Any place is a good place to start. It just depends upon your objective for studying. If you are interested in practical Christian living, read the writings of Paul and the other apostles. If you want to know more about the life of Christ, read the gospels. You may be interested in Bible history and if so, start with the Old Testament. It's all good and good for you.

Do I always have to study the Bible?

Of course not. You may find that you just want to read the Bible to become more familiar with it. I do this quite often and have found that it sometimes directs me to a course of study, but most often not. Whether you are just reading or studying, they both will prove profitable.

How should I prepare myself for time in the word?

Pray before you start. Ask the Lord to direct you in your choice of what to read. Pray that He will open up your understanding and give you wisdom concerning what you read. Expect Him to speak to your heart as you read the word. Sometimes as you read the Bible, you will be drawn to a certain Scripture verse or maybe just a phrase. When you have that experience, God is usually highlighting that verse for you to pause and reflect on it.

Do you have any advice on how to approach a Bible study?

Ask questions as you read. Some appropriate questions would be:
- How would I explain what I read in my own words?
- Who is speaking in the Scripture?
- Does this Scripture reveal anything to me about God?

- Does it reveal anything to me about myself?
- What is the main point of what I read?
- How is what I read relevant to me?

Try seeing the Scripture as well as reading it. Ponder on some of the words and see what pictures come to mind. This helps to increase your understanding of what you have read and brings the Bible to life.

Some Final Thoughts on Bible Study

Prayer. Pray before and after you read or study. Ask God to help you live your life in the light of what you just read.

Take notes. Take notes on what you read. Keep a pen and notebook or journal with you as you study. You may want to write down something that spoke directly to you, something you want to study in more detail or some question you would like to discuss with someone.

Be consistent. Try to be consistent in when you read the Bible and the amount of time you will allow. Of course, there will be some variation depending on whatever else is going on in your life. The main idea is that you carve out a time for Bible Study and try to stick with it.

Application. This is where you take what you have read and apply it to the everyday routine of your life. For example, if the Bible tells you not to lie, then in a situation where you would be tempted to fudge on the truth, you remember that word and you pray for grace and strength to do what it says. Application is simply taking the attitude of obedience that says, "What the Bible says, I will do." With this attitude of heart you will discover God's grace and strength will be there for you.